Horseback Journeys of Celia Fiennes

1000 Miles Across England

Horseback Journeys of Celia Fiennes

1000 Miles Across England

Elizabeth Barrett

Wimpole Books
Kenton, Suffolk

First published in Great Britain by

Wimpole Books, Kenton, Stowmarket, Suffolk

1992

To Bill & Cameron and to all who helped make it possible

(front cover photo) The author riding Cameron along the Tissington Trail

Cover design, painting of Celia Fiennes on Rowan and map of routes by Anne Grahame Johnstone

Photographs by Bill, Elizabeth & Philip Barrett

Sketches by Philip Barrett

Chapter "The Times of William & Mary " by Sara Coveley

British Library Cataloguing in Publication Data

Barrett, Elizabeth Ann

Horseback Journeys of Celia Fiennes : 1000 miles across England

I. Title

914.20468

ISBN 0 951 6011 1 3

Printed in Great Britain by The Witney Press Ltd, Witney, Oxford

Contents

Contents

Preface

Towards the end of the seventeenth century the determined, resourceful and courageous Celia Fiennes undertook the adventure of riding round "most parts" of England, rides that were to cover thousands of miles. She recorded her journeyings daily in her diary, which now provides an invaluable source of guidance and information about the times: an all-important piece of social and factual history.

Elizabeth Barrett in this book sets out to recreate the Northern Journey and the East Anglian section of the Great Journey of Celia.

Sadly Celia tells us little about the horses that she rode during her journeys; fortunately Elizabeth Barrett is less restrained and we warm to her somewhat unpredictable chesnut with the unlikely name of Marbeck Cameron.

If we ask ourselves what was travelling in England like in the seventeenth century, the answer can only be extremely uncomfortable and often dangerous. Celia tells us of various misadventures, of how she nearly drowned in the flooded causeway near Ely, how her horse fell in a bad hole in the wood in Devon, of encounters with highwaymen. Elizabeth Barrett has followed Celia's route as nearly as she can and in so doing has proved that it is still possible to travel round much of England on little frequented bridleways and quiet roads.

In following Celia's route Elizabeth Barrett's lively account recreates the sights and situations described by Celia almost three hundred years before. In arriving at Newby Hall near Ripon, Celia much admired the gardens "full of borders with flowers and green banks with flower pots". A present day traveller to Newby finds a garden no less exciting and the house, as then, of the greatest distinction "built with brick and coyn'd with stone ... " or to Chatsworth where Celia comments on a large park and several fine gardens " ... and in the middle of each garden is a large fountain full of images Sea Gods and Dolphins and Sea Horses which are full of pipes which spout out water in the bason and spouts all about the gardens ...". The Sea Gods and Dolphins are still there to be marvelled at today.

A justly favourite travel journal is Stevenson's "Travels with a Donkey" in the Cevennes - famed for its beauty of the descriptive writing, for the magic he brings to the sights and sounds around him. Celia in contrast wrote with no sense of style, with little attention to grammar, spelling or punctuation. She aims not for beauty or magic, facts are her stock-in-trade and it is the facts that we find so engrossing.

Celia encourages us with the instruction that ''persons should spend time in journeys to visit their native land and to be curious and inform themselves ... of pleasant prospects, and good buildings''. She adds that travellers ''would cure the evil itch of over valuing foreign parts'' - though it is hard to imagine that many members of the people of this country in the seventeenth century would even have had the chance of visiting ''foreign parts''!

Elizabeth Barrett does much to convince us that there is so much to interest us and to engage our attention in England that we too should busy ourselves in following in Celia's steps, preferably no doubt on a horse but if not then on foot or by bicycle or indeed by car.

This book has encouraged me to re-acquaint myself more fully with the diary of my illustrious ancestor Celia Fiennes. My hope is that many others may share something of my pleasure by reading this book and then by feeling led back to the original diary.

Saye

Broughton Castle

June 1992

Introduction

In this tercentenary year of William and Mary it is worth recalling how many changes they brought with them across the North Sea. The events of 1688/9 constituted an historic watershed. Monarchs and parliament were enabled to develop new relationships so that over the years the Westminster form of parliamentary government could develop. William and Mary, one might say, gave back to the nation its self-confidence. A divided nation on the edge of Europe - how topical this all sounds - became one of the great European powers and a lasting friendship with The Netherlands was established.

Through the country at this time rode the daughter of a Cromwellian colonel, Celia Fiennes. She rode to improve her health and her mind and made notes along the way. The result is a fascinating and unique record of the country at the end of the seventeenth century, following the Civil War and at the time of great change which came in its wake.

She was born on 7 June 1662 and was 20 when she first began her journeyings; the early ones were carried out with her mother, often visiting relations and a few of the journeys may have been by carriage. She was 35 when she set off on her northern tour, on horseback and possibly accompanied by her nieces Susanna & Mary Filmer who lived at Amwellbury in Hertfordshire. It is thought that she also took at least two servants with her and her hound. Unfortunately she does not describe the horses which they rode but they were most likely to have been about 15 hands (1 hand = 4 inches) and could possibly have been part bred Arabs as a large number of Arab stallions was being imported during the latter part of the seventeenth century. To have faced the various hazards of travelling in that time, the horses - and the riders - would have had to have been bold and to have had plenty of stamina. It is likely also that she took spare riding horses and a pack horse but on the mechanics of her journeyings she has little to say. The most that she says is that she completed a journey with no falls. At the end of the northern journey she says "I returned all our Company, Blessed be God, very well without any disaster or trouble in 7 weeks and Tyme".

She frequented spas, which was becoming fashionable, and was an astute observer of all that she saw. She was a staunch Nonconformist at a time when the Act of Toleration had only just become law. She attended as many Nonconformist meetings as she could, often travelling many miles over difficult terrain to do so.

Sadly there is no known portrait of her but this is thought to be because single ladies were not regarded as of great importance and so it was not the custom for portraits of them to be painted. We have no full knowledge of how she dressed. She wore a duster coat - a light top coat - for travelling and, from our knowledge of the costume of the time, it is likely that she would have also worn a full or divided skirt. The rest of her garb would have been similar to that worn by men - boots, jacket and hat.

What I sought to do was recreate the Northern Journey and also the East Anglian section of the Great Journey. There were two facets to this re-creation in my mind. The first was the challenge of riding a horse for long distances around twentieth century England, keeping to quiet lanes, byways and bridleways, and avoiding busy roads. The second was to compare the England which Celia saw with the England of today. It hardly needs saying that travel on horseback in the 1980s has associated with it a wholly different set of hazards from those which Celia encountered.

However, there were times when I felt an uplifting sense that nothing had changed, when for instance I realised that the houses which I was looking at would have been seen by Celia or when I emerged into a village such as Bury Green near Bishops Stortford which is still as it must have looked then - with a cluster of houses around the green used for grazing or recreation and even with a modern bungalow tucked neatly away just out of sight, as if deliberately.

My modus operandi was to ride my eight year old part-bred Welsh Cob gelding of 16 hands. In some parts of the country it is still possible to ride without backup using saddlebags for one's luggage. However, in trying to keep as near as possible to Celia's route I could not locate sufficient stabling and accommodation to enable me to do this. For the northern ride, therefore, I had a backup horse trailer so that I could obtain a lift to my next night's stabling when necessary and also so that I could bypass sections which were impracticable to ride.

My horse, Marbeck Cameron, has been with me since a foal. After eight years he is still unpredictable, a complete clown who is just as likely to stand with his forefeet crossed like a Disney cartoon horse as to stand correctly. If one stands on a bank to mount him, he is likely to try and climb the bank himself, making the whole exercise very difficult. But, having said all that, he has innumerable virtues, the chief one of which is that he will settle at once in strange surroundings and so feeding him is never a problem on tour. However, he is chesnut and often displays the temperament to go with that colour, chesnuts being the redheads of the horse world. He is the successor to my previous Welsh Cob, Rowan, with whom I began the re-creation of the Great

Journey a few years ago.

Rowan died suddenly of a tear in the intestinal wall support the day we were going to travel to Ely and then on northwards to Wansford. He was completely different from Cameron, being red roan in colour with a flaxen mane and tail. He stood at just over 15 hands, and was extremely bold, keen and very powerful. Unusually, he was five gaited, meaning that he could amble in addition to walking, trotting, cantering and galloping. The amble is extremely comfortable and at this pace I could travel for miles at a steady seven or eight miles an hour. The great similarity between the two horses is that Cameron, just as Rowan before him, regards any outing as a gastronomic affair. He is ready to graze or to browse in hedgerows at any opportunity, or indeed to create that opportunity. The sudden loss of Rowan, who had been with us ten years, was not only a personal tragedy but it also caused a gap in the Celia Fiennes venture. The East Anglian section was ridden entirely on Rowan.

The route which I followed was as close as practicable to the route which I believe Celia followed, using old roads and bridleways wherever possible. I avoided busy town centres for reasons of safety and practicality - I was not setting out to make any kind of point but merely to observe and, of course, to enjoy the ride. For this reason I started the ride just north of London and terminated it on the return leg at St Albans.

A further comment on the roads which Celia used is probably appropriate. Some were Roman, such as Ermine Street - these were known as the King's Highways because they were protected by Royal Charter - and some were ridgeways, probably dating back to Neolithic times. My route took in part of the Icknield Way, ridgeways and some pilgrims' routes. Celia would have also used portways - that is the ways to and from market towns or ''ports'' and many drovers' roads - hog ways, salt ways and so on.

When Celia rode there were few carriages in use in the countryside; most people rode or walked and goods were carried by pack ponies or horses. Pickfords, who are still of course in the transport business, were operating then. Celia would have met on her travels many herds of animals and flocks of birds being driven to market; typical routes were from Wales and East Anglia to London. Pigs would travel at around six miles a day and geese much less. Geese were sometimes shod or walked through tar and sand to prevent their feet getting sore and consequently slowing the rate of travel. My aim was to cover a similar distance daily to that which Celia records.

Journeys of Celia Fiennes 1697 re-created in 1983, 1988 & 1991
North Sea
Scarborough
Ripon
Boroughbridge
Knaresborough
Harrogate
York
Tadcaster
Pontefract
Doncaster
Blyth
Castleton
Worksop
Lincoln
Buxton
Chesterfield
Mansfield
Newark
Uttoxeter
Wolseley
Nottingham
Grantham
Lichfield
Stretton
Stamford
Peterborough
Norwich
Blythburgh
Coventry
Bury St. Edmunds
Warwick
Northampton
Stony Stratford
Cambridge
Ipswich
Broughton
Woburn
Audley End
Chipping Norton
Bishops Stortford
Dunstable
Amwell
St. Albans
Lambourn
London
Newton Tony

Part I

Setting the Scene

1

The Times of William & Mary

The seventeenth century was a time of political upheaval and social change. By the end of the century the English had developed for themselves a system of parliamentary government and local administration. A new parliamentary England emerged as the House of Commons under the leadership of the squires in alliance with merchants established itself as the governing organ of a modern nation. The political and religious tyranny of the monarch had effectively been curbed. The reign of William and Mary established permanently a freely elected parliament, trial by independent jury, freedom to practise religious beliefs and freedom of speech.

In 1685 a young woman called Celia Fiennes set out on the first of many journeys round Britain. By 1705 she had covered almost the whole length of the country, recording all her adventures in a fascinating journal which creates a vivid picture of seventeenth century England.

Cecilia Fiennes, or Celia as she was always known, was born in June 1662 at Newton Toney near Salisbury. Her father was Col Nathaniel Fiennes, second son of the First Viscount Saye and Sele. Her mother, Frances, was the daughter of a Roundhead colonel, Richard Whitehead. Celia was brought up in a strongly Puritan household, her political opinions were decidedly Whiggish. Celia's family was spread all over the country, many of them country squires and merchants - so she found little difficulty in moving between social spheres. She first acquired her interest in travel as a young woman in the 1680s when she embarked upon many journeys with her mother who took her to relatives in the south, to Bath, Oxford and Winchester. After the death of her mother in 1691 Celia undertook a few tours from London to visit relatives, travelling to Hampshire and Surrey.

In 1697 she set out on her most ambitious journey yet, at the age of 35 she left London on horseback on the start of a northern tour which took her to Cambridge, Lincoln and Scarborough and back via Buxton, Warwick and St Albans. She did the journey in seven weeks and was able to visit Kent that same summer. A year later her enthusiasm undampened she set out once again, her second journey taking her from Norfolk to Newcastle, Carlisle to North Wales and down to Land's End.

Celia gives few details of her travel arrangements, she travelled mostly alone with one or two servants and spare horses, as well as a greyhound which she mentions briefly. It is likely that her nieces, Mary and Susanna Filmer who lived at Amwellbury in Hertfordshire, accompanied her on part if not all of the Northern Journey. Celia mentions that she carried her bed linen with her, obviously she was aware of the lack of hygiene in most country inns.

She was an observant person and kept a journal in which she meticulously recorded everything that she saw. Few diaries exist from Stuart times and those kept by women generally record domestic affairs. Celia kept a travel diary in which she wrote about England from a woman's viewpoint. She travelled the length and breadth of England and her diary is the first comprehensive journal of that kind since the reign of Elizabeth I.

Celia gave the reason for her journeys as the wish to regain her health by variety and change. She suggested that others should undertake such a course of action to expand their horizons and expand their health "with a hearty wish and a recommendation to all but especially to my own sex, the study of those things which tend to improve the mind and makes our life pleasant and comfortable as well as profitable in all stages and stations".

Celia's journals are written in an enthusiastic and flowing style, keenly describing all that she observed. Her style and grammar are erratic, she quotes historical "facts" which are often inaccurate. She showed great interest in the countryside and nature, in industry and especially mining, in gardens and houses.

As a Puritan, she was always matter of fact with almost unromantic tastes and virtues. She admired the utilitarian and up to date. She was a solemn and proper young woman; she found the paintings in Lord Exeter's apartments at Burghley immodest and was censorious of Scottish peasants whom she found lazy. Celia showed genuine social concern about sanitation and living conditions, she thought the rows at Chester were unhealthy! Yet she found great delight in all she saw and was the ideal tourist, she was unsceptical, intrigued by curiosities and went out of her way to see strange objects. At the press in Oxford she could not resist printing her name. At Bury St Edmunds an apothecary "showed me a curiosity of a herball all written out with every sort of herb and tree dried and cut out and pasted on the leaves". She climbed up cathedral towers, visited the dissecting rooms at Newcastle surgeons' hall. She returned home with many souvenirs of her travels, a Cornish diamond, jet from Wigan, a piece of copper from Derbyshire. Celia was a determined woman of independent spirit. Travel in the seventeenth century was dangerous and uncomfortable, the English countryside was often inhospitable. It took a strong

Puritan desire for self-improvement, a sense of adventure and her insatiable curiosity to set off on her journeys. Celia remained unflustered by whatever happened. The weather seldom deterred her and she was even unperturbed by a confrontation with two highwaymen.

The effect of her journeys is to create for us a panorama of England. In the seventeenth century the population of England and Wales was between four and four and half million. London was not the focus of English life. The counties had more autonomous powers as communications were rudimentary and roads appalling. Members of parliament and lord lieutenants of counties travelled to London infrequently. England was a rich, populous, thriving country at peace after the political and religious tensions. There was an expansion in commerce and the beginnings of an industrial revolution as well as changes in agriculture. Four fifths of the population was engaged in agriculture and England was essentially rural. Half the arable land was farmed in strips in the open field system although there were important pockets of manufacture and industry. The open field system, preferable for the cottagers and labourers, worked side by side with enclosed farms. English agriculture was rich and varied, which pleased Celia. The richest counties were Middlesex, Devonshire and Somerset. Kent was the most highly cultivated; known as the Garden of England, it produced hops and fruits as did Worcestershire and Herefordshire. The eastern half of England produced grain and was involved in fishing, sheep rearing, shipbuilding and wool and textiles. Sheep and cattle were fattened on turnips in Suffolk. The west was good for pasturage, cattle and sheep farming.

Every village and small town had local craftsmen and specialist rural industries. The manufacture of textiles was one of the most important. Celia described Peterborough as a "very industrious thriving town" with "spinning and knitting amongst the ordinary people".

Farming was becoming a capitalist enterprise and land was in great demand. During the seventeenth century the Fens were drained since reclaimed soil was very rich. The development of the three field rotation system or up and down husbandry increased soil fertility. It was practised on enclosed farms and led to a more efficient use of land. Cattle and sheep farming was concentrated on areas unsuitable for arable farming. But by the end of the seventeenth century more than half the cultivated land still lay in green fields and communal husbandry was still largely practised.

Celia took a great interest in industry and reported all that she saw in detail such as the production of serge in Exeter. She was fascinated by industrial developments and processes. The manufacture of textiles was well established and was becoming more diversified. The linen industry was developing in Lancashire and there was an active woollen industry. The mining of coal extended north through the Midlands as output rose substantially. Celia was interested in all aspects of mining, she observed miners at work at Buxton; "they digg down their mines like a well", visited tin mines in Cornwall, copper mines and at Beaudesert saw coal being drawn up. Salt was an important commodity and Celia took particular note since she had financial interests. In the later seventeenth century other new industries emerged and Celia described paper making, silk, lace and pottery manufacture. The limited monarchy which resulted from the 1688 revolution ensured that powerful economic interests in the community could exert their influence over government policy.

It was the period of the large country house and thanks to Celia we have descriptions of many grand homes. After the Restoration many architects returned to England with European ideas. There was a new spurt in design yet the style remained typically English. Dutch influence meant that brick and stone became fashionable: at Coleshill "the house is new built with stone".

The raftered hall became unfashionable and the various purposes of the old hall were divided up. The dining and drawing rooms were built on the first storey and the central feature of old manor houses, the courtyard, disappeared. The Earl of Clarendon's rectangular classical house designed for him by Roger Pratt set a trend in domestic building. The square classical shape enshrined in the Queen Anne style of graceful pillars and regular facades became popular. As glass became cheaper large windows became an important feature of a gentleman's house. Sash windows were invented and high well-lighted rooms became fashionable.

The hall was now a room of entry with a sweeping staircase leading to the upstairs rooms. Staircases and landings were broad and balustrades elaborately carved. Jacobean panelling was replaced with tapestries (Celia particularly liked embroideries and tapestries), hangings and wall paintings. Elaborate plasterwork was popular. Rushes were replaced by carpets and matting, and carpets were imported from Turkey and Persia. Furniture became more elegant and less heavy and oak was replaced by walnut.

Chairs, cabinets and stools were lighter and more attractively designed. Chinaware was brought to Europe by the Dutch and the East Indies companies. Celia had a very distinct idea about houses, she had no interest in the old, eg Haddon Hall and Penshurst. She preferred the London "mode" and liked Lord Chesterfield's house at Bradby. "Ye front have something surprising in it, it is all free stone which is dipt in oil .... that adds a varnish to its lustre."

Celia liked beautiful furnishings, and at Lord Orfford's house she noted "in ye best drawing roome was a very Rich hanging, gold and silver and little scarlet; mostly tissue and brocade of gold and silver".

The reign of William and Mary signified a period of change, new wealth and nobility gave rise to new buildings and gardens. Daniel Defoe praised William for reviving an interest in gardens. Celia was enthusiastic about the gardens which she saw and she shared her taste for the neat and tidy with her contemporaries. She admired Sir Ralph Verney's garden for being "most exact". It was the age of the English garden. Vast tracts of land were turned into parks and large gardens. Terraces, lakes and other water features soon became popular.

At first gardens had been uninspiring geometric patterns with tall trees and shrubs. But under the influence of William and Mary gardens became more imaginative; radiating avenues, arcades of trees and flower filled borders soon became popular. The tradition of the formal garden had begun and Celia witnessed this as she travelled through England. She took note of fine walks and flowers in the garden; at Coleshill she noted "all the avenues to the house are fine walkes of rows of trees....of many steps and terraces and gravel walks with all sorts of dwarf trees, fruit trees". She described in detail the design of gardens and liked everything new, she was particularly fond of grottoes and hydraulic jests. At Wilton near Salisbury there was a grotto "garnished with many fine figures of ye goddesses" and at Bretby a water clock. At Chatsworth Celia recorded terraced walks and fir groves, she admired the seahorse fountain, the Triton fountain and the cascade.

At Newby Hall and Burghley Celia describes statues, cut work hedges, exotic plants, avenues of Scots, Norway and fir pines. She tells us about parterres and fruit gardens, gooseberries, cherries, apricots and plums which were all known in the seventeenth century. At Woburn she wrote "in the square just by the dining room window is all sorts of pots of flowers and curious greens, fine orange citron and lemon trees".

Most gardens had flowers in borders, knots, scroll parterres or separate hedged gardens. She particularly liked roses, stocks and honeysuckles. She tells us that yew, bay and myrtle trees were used for topiary work (there were new opportunities for obtaining plants through trade with the East Indies). Her descriptions bring to life gardens which remain only in paintings due to the eighteenth century fashion for natural landscaping.

In late Stuart England it had become very popular to visit spas for one's health; there was widespread belief that they could offer cures for all manner of complaints. The new fashion for taking the waters began when Dudley,

Third Baron North, discovered the waters at Tunbridge. The waters of Bath were beginning to attract the nobility while Buxton and Harrogate were frequented by northern gentry. Epsom and Tunbridge Wells soon became fashionable resorts as more than a hundred mineral springs were promoted for their health giving properties and resorts soon developed around the springs. Tunbridge Wells boasted plenty of good lodgings, a chapel, shops and coffee houses. Buxton however remained well known for its poor lodgings.

Celia followed the trend for taking the waters and was quite an authority on the various properties of each spa. She compared dietetic waters with sulphurous and noted the amounts of alum and steel present, being almost scientific in her approach. In many places the water was unpalatable, full of dirt and leaves; at Barnet she could not face drinking the waters and at Harrogate her horse refused to go near the spring. Celia was fussy about bathing as near as possible to the actual spring and she gives an intriguing account how a lady should take the waters without losing her modesty.

As well as visiting the spas she enjoyed sampling local specialities; she certainly had a healthy appetite and writes with zest about the food which she tried. In seventeenth century England the diet consisted largely of meat and bread made from rye. Fish and meat were preserved using spices and salt, an important commodity. Fruit and vegetables were not eaten in quantities, although they could be grown in cottage plots. Cheese and eggs were eaten and milk was drunk watered down. Pepper, cinnamon, cloves, nutmeg and ginger were all important spices. Beer was the universal drink of the Englishman and was made from wheat, oats, barley, rye or millet, being brewed on estates or at home. Celia was something of a connoisseur of beer and she also enjoyed French wine when it could be obtained. Tea, coffee and spirits were available only to the wealthy. In Westmorland Celia saw oat clapbread being made "they mixed their flour with water, so soft to rowle it in their hands in a ball". In Cornwall she ate west country tart "apple pye with Custard all on top". At Woburn she sampled a quantity of Red Coralina gooseberry. She had potted char at Windermere, bought a salmon in Scotland and ate plenty of oysters in Colchester.

Part II

The Northern Journey of 1697

Ridden on Cameron in 1988

2

Broxbourne to Bishop's Stortford

After five years of waiting and planning I could hardly believe that I was about to set off on my great adventure. I had chosen to begin my ride north of London at Broxbourne in Hertfordshire, along a section of Ermine Street. My eager sense of anticipation had been transmitted to Cameron and he was fidgeting and fussing as I tacked him up. Then, as I prepared to mount, other riders appeared and I had great difficulty in getting him to stand still at all. Eventually I managed to clamber on from the ramp of the trailer and at last I was off, but still struggling with my map case and gloves - not the text-book way of beginning a ride but no matter we were headed north.

I began to look around and noted that the track was wide but deeply rutted, bounded in part by trees and, as we progressed, by farmland and the large beech trees were reminiscent of parts of Kent. Cameron had by now settled into his stride and we were really beginning to get going. I thought about travel in pre-eighteenth century England when the highways leading to and from London were often impassable in winter and occasionally at other times too because of floods and were consequently in a state of deep mud which made travel extremely difficult. The condition was made worse by the constant passage of driven beasts and animals and the incessant stream of pack horses and galloping post horses.

My thoughts were brought back to the present quickly, however, as I was starting my ride after the wettest winter on record and this stretch of Ermine Street was extremely deep in mud. We plunged from one muddy section to the next and I got through only by dint of riding a large, powerful and willing horse - many horses would have been reluctant to keep going. Even Cameron floundered and came close to giving up - I thought to myself "What a way to start a ride". At one moment I was pushed heavily against a tree and before negotiating the first ford I dismounted to find the easiest way across. Cameron gamely followed me and I remounted and bit by bit we began to get going again. Some of the deep ruts were, I suspect, caused by four wheel drive vehicles but the sense of re-creating the time of Celia Fiennes was nonetheless very strong. I paused at the end of that section of Ermine Street to see if all Cameron's shoes were intact - luckily they were but then I glanced at myself and found that I was literally covered in mud. It looked just as if I had fallen at the muddiest section but the mud had all been flung up to bespatter me. I continued, hoping that the mud would soon dry on both of us and that the worst was behind us.

Fortunately the going did change dramatically. From the mud of Ermine Street we were now in suburbia and much to my surprise a young girl was trotting towards me on a small pony along a busy road. My immediate reaction was that she was too young to be out unaccompanied - an adult on a bicycle would have made for greater safety. The route next took us through the grounds of Haileybury, the public school which was founded a century and a half after Celia's ride. A park surrounds the school and through it flows the New River created by Hugh Myddleton, whose inspiration it was to carry water from these chalk hills to the London of Stuart times. There is a monument to him nearby.

We went on to Amwellbury just south of Ware, Celia's first stopping place. The house was then owned by a relative Thomas Filmer, a London lawyer, the father of Susanna and Mary who it is believed accompanied her on this journey. The house is about 20 miles from London and one presumes that he also had a London house in order to practise there as a lawyer. Amwellbury still stands in its own grounds and with a lodge on the road which is the old A10, now bypassed. A bridleway runs close to the house, a route which Celia would perforce have used.

From Amwellbury the route took us on towards Ware, then on to Wareside. During the whole of this section I noted the large number of horses and ponies in fields and also being ridden. The bridleways were also well signed and open - no doubt a result of the pressure created by the many riders in this part of Hertfordshire. We had the opportunity for some good steady trots and a few canters. Drivers of motor vehicles encountered on the road were almost invariably courteous, no doubt again the result of the amount of horse traffic on these roads. Our route took us to Baker's End and through to Much Hadham. I was pleased to find that surfaces had improved a great deal since the earlier section.

The attractive village of Much Hadham, with its many timber-framed and thatched houses which Celia could well have seen, looked even more attractive from my viewpoint nine feet above the ground as I was able to appreciate the gardens which would normally be hidden from sight. This village was the country home of the bishops of London for eight hundred years and in a farmhouse nearby the widow of Henry V gave birth to Edmund Tudor. He won the throne on Bosworth field which Celia visited and which I intended to visit also. This was very much a journey through time and another link with the history of England was that a one-time rector, Alexander Nowell, wrote the

Catechism.

The countryside through which we were travelling was expansive and beautiful, hilly with open fields, well-defined woods and hedges. This was quite astonishing as I was so near London and so near encroaching suburbia - the ''rust'' described by E M Forster in ''Howard's End'' which was set in this very area.

At Much Hadham we forded the River Ash and Cameron stopped for a long drink: with so many fords en route there was no problem with watering. Some children on bicycles were having fun splashing through but Cameron was too absorbed in drinking to pay attention to them. The next bridleway, to Bury Green, was beside a stream through large inviting grass fields which were just right for a steady canter. Although Cameron had had a long day and was at this stage only partially fit, he could not resist putting in two big bucks and a swerve to the right, nearly depositing me on the grass. This habit of his is difficult to stop and equally difficult to deal with. It makes one yearn to know more about the horses which Celia used, as one can hardly imagine her riding a horse anything like Cameron and living so dangerously. Furthermore, unruly behaviour in horses is infectious and if her horse had played up the rest of the party, and all other riders in the vicinity, could have easily been in chaos. Although one has to bear in mind that generally the more work which a horse is given, the steadier it becomes.

The only thing which marred my pleasure on this stretch was the need to dismount and undo numerous gates. In times past the elderly country doctor or clergyman going about his business would not have expected to dismount to open and shut gates: of necessity it would have been made easy to work them from horseback. There should really be no problem today as it is as easy to erect a gate which can be opened from a horse's back as one which can not but, in fairness, it would have been easier for me to mount and dismount if Cameron had been a smaller horse.

Thence to Bishop's Stortford. We had travelled some eighteen miles - long and difficult miles as Celia would have described them - and my horse and I finished the ride covered in mud and in a worse state than I could recall in many decades of riding. Celia describes the town as ''a very pretty neat Market town a good Church and a delicate Spring of Water which has a wall built round it very sweet and cleare water for drinking, there is a little river runns by the town which feeds severall Mills''. It was with a sense of satisfaction that I completed the first day of our long journey.

THE POST-ROADS OF ENGLAND, 1675. —— DIRECT ROADS - - - - CROSS ROADS

3

Bishop's Stortford to Cambridge

Suffering no ill effects from the previous day's ride and having cleaned up and dried out I set forth on a mild day in watery sunshine. I crossed the Stort at Manuden over a pack-bridge and climbed the hills, following bridleways which were all well marked and easy to find. This was part of a newly created recreational route called the Harcamlow Way which passes through two counties. The going was much easier and the tracks sandy; at last we could get out of a walk and enjoyed several canters. The word ''canter'' by the way is an historical reminder as it comes from ''Canterbury gallop'' the pace at which Chaucer's pilgrims were said to have progressed. Part of our route ran parallel to the M11, the London to Cambridge motorway, but within sight of this twentieth century creation I was pleased to encounter several deer in a wood. Cameron on this occasion simply gave a couple of snorts and a prance, and then carried on steadily. One always wonders whether one will be deposited on the ground by the fearfully big bucks which he is capable of producing with very little warning.

It was sad to come across the remains of a timber cross-winged house, although whether this was the result of the recent hurricane or of total neglect, or indeed of both, I was unable to tell. A little later I came to another large green, Ricking Green, with some modern houses around but well designed so as not to detract from the scene. This green had been mowed for cricket, a game which Celia might have seen played although she makes few references to any games in her journals. Various games were being played in her time. Bowls, for instance, was popular and Cornwall was noted for its hurling matches which were played between parishes with a ball against the churchyard wall. The matches were announced by the town crier carrying a silver plated ball. In Yorkshire they had Easter Monday sports of stoolball and other games at Clark Bridge, Halifax, which were enjoyed by hundreds of young and old in churchyards and on village greens.

As I approached the M11 I could hear the continuous roar of traffic and I began to feel slightly apprehensive in case I had to cross by a bridge. However, as I neared the motorway I could see that our route took us under it and well away from the noise. Nearing Newport, football was being played in a field beside the track and Cameron was more worked up by watching the ball being kicked around than by the traffic on the motorway. Newport, by the way, is one of the commonest place names in the country because it is linked to the use of the word "port" for market town commented on earlier. From Newport, crossing my first ford of the day, I made my way by bridleway towards Littlebury, passing underneath the motorway again. This is so much easier than crossing by bridge as the noise of traffic is shut off with dramatic suddenness as one enters the tunnel. The landscape had now changed, with large rolling hills and expansive views, reflecting the chalk which lay beneath.

It was easier to visit Audley End without Cameron, especially as I had made no prior arrangement to take him there. In Celia's time the house belonged to the Earl of Sussex and it was so vast that it gave the appearance of a town. The present house, now substantially reduced in size, stands on the site of the medieval abbey of Walden. In her time it was the largest Jacobean house ever built and was a palace for Charles II, who was attracted because of its nearness to Newmarket. However, the King's enthusiasm for the house waned and it became almost totally neglected from 1688. So at the time of Celia's ride in 1697 decay was evident. I was impressed with the great hall and with Winstanley's drawing of the house as she saw it but, perhaps overly influenced by Celia's description, was disappointed in the appearance of the house and gardens.

There were no gardens to speak of and the house had much changed from the Jacobean house with formal gardens which Celia would have seen. The gardens were landscaped a century later by Sir John Griffin Griffin, later Lord Howard, to a design of Capability Brown. However, one can still see the ha-ha and the house is beautifully situated with a temple on the high land behind it.

Wansford Bridge

At Littlebury lived Henry Winstanley who designed the first Eddystone lighthouse and perished when it was destroyed in a storm. He also executed drawings of large houses and there is a set of Audley End in the library there. He advertised this service -

"...All Noble men and Gentlemen that please to have their Mansion Houses design'd on Copper Plates, to be printed for composeing a volume of ye Prospects of ye Principall Houses of England; may have them done by........ Mr Henry Winstanley by way of subscription..."

I enquired around the village but was unable to locate his house or discover whether it still existed. The oldest inhabitant knew of Winstanley but could not help with his house. In the event the answer was quite simply that it had long since been demolished and the only trace of it was a mound by the churchyard. There was a sense of loss as Winstanley was a man of many parts and, although Celia did not meet him, she was fascinated by the house with its clockwork displays. One of the inventions which brought many visitors to the house was "the chaire .... which runs backwards into the garden on a rail". Winstanley also had a water theatre in which tea and coffee were laid on in pipes and cups presented to the company. At the close all the pipes threw jets of water.

I had travelled another nineteen miles in Celia's footsteps. She obviously rode up what is now the A11, the route being based on a Roman road. My route, however, took me via Strethall to Great Chesterford. This section is part of the proposed Icknield Way long distance path for riders and walkers. The track to Great Chesterford is waymarked and I simply followed the track and then the hedge until we reached the motorway again. This time we went over the motorway by bridleway bridge: this was much less pleasant than going underneath as the noise was horrific, akin to standing on a high board in a crowded swimming pool, and Cameron was frightened. A fast trot was the only safe speed; however, he calms down quickly and he was settled by the time we reached the railway line. Thankfully there were no trains about. One recalls Black Beauty's description of her first encounter with a train ".. I shall never forget the first train that ran by, I was feeding quietly near the pales which separated the meadow from the railway, when I heard a strange sound in the distance, and before I knew whence it came - with a rush and a clatter, and a puffing out of smoke. A long black train of something flew by .... I turned and galloped to the further side of the meadow as fast as I could go, and there I stood snorting with astonishment and fear .... I found that this terrible creature never came into our field...." The description takes me back to when I was a young child. I used to help at the local stables and one of my holiday or Saturday morning jobs was to take the ponies to be shod. On my way I used to cross the railway by a bridge and if there was a train there, especially if it was getting up steam, the ponies would prance and jump around and I was always thankful when I was safely past.

I went on into Great Chesterford with its attractive timber-framed buildings. This was the starting point for an interesting but short-lived railway development in the middle of the nineteenth century, when the Jockey Club supported a private venture to build a line to Newmarket. The thinking was that it would enable more people to participate in racing and would also enable members of Parliament to return to London the same day to take part in the evening's debate, but sadly the line closed within a few years.

Our route took us north-east towards Linton on a good wide track but it totally disappeared within the woods and it was quite difficult in places to push our way through, with Cameron twisting and turning through the trees and his feet slipping and sliding on the now narrow path. Eventually we were safely through and the way widened out as we approached Linton. I went into the delightful village with its excellent home-made pie and cake shop, where such delicacies as umble pie and apple strudels were on sale.

The villages in this valley were Roman and Saxon settlements which grew up close together because of the ready availability of water and one can today see several villages at one time. Indeed, Celia commented on the neat villages, rows of trees and the number of churches which could be seen. This landscape has not changed substantially and we were delighted at Babraham to find the house of Sir Richard Bennett as she described it, still with a fine avenue of trees. The house is now occupied by the Animal Physiology Unit of the Agricultural Research Council. Although the park still has a large number of sheep, they are penned into small areas with high chainlink fencing all around. This fencing may be effective but it does, unfortunately, rather spoil the effect of open parkland.

Bourn Bridge, which Celia comments on, is close by on the A11 road. It is no more than just a bridge and it is doubtful whether it was any more than that in Celia's time. It was an early settlement of which trace has disappeared. She took a special interest in bridges and her comments may be an example of that interest. From the village of Linton we climbed up to the Via Devana, or Wool Street, a Roman or earlier road which she most likely used. This may be a section of an important route between Colchester and Chester. The road remains unmetalled between Haverhill and Cambridge, as does the Gartree Road near Leicester which I later intended to ride. The name Wool Street comes not from wool but from ''wolves'' and the road was indeed known to be very dangerous because it was infested with wolves. One notes a similar origin in the place name Woolpit in Suffolk, which is derived from "wolf pit".

I rode on the wide track with the agger evident in many places. The going was a little slippery underfoot but the riding was most enjoyable with views to both north and south over the rolling mainly arable countryside. I soon reached Wandlebury Fort on the Gog Magog Hills, a most impressive but much altered iron age fort which Celia noted. These chalk hills take their name from the two gods of English folklore who are said to be buried in the vicinity. Giant figures were once cut into the hillside and were visible up to the end of the eighteenth century. There was work done in the mid-twentieth century to seek to uncover these figures but the results were inconclusive. The figure of a horse and chariot was said to have been uncovered but there is nothing to be seen now.

On the site of the fort King James built a hunting lodge; later the place passed into the hands of Earl Godolphin, the owner of the famous Godolphin Barb. All thoroughbred horses trace their ancestry back to this horse and another horse the Darley Arabian. The Godolphin Barb is indeed buried under the archway of the stable block at Wandlebury and a gravestone marks the spot. The horse was 29 when he died, a good age to achieve. It has to be borne in mind that the three hundred years of history which we are considering take us back to before the time when the thoroughbred horse existed. The breed, which has become almost synonymous with the word "horse" in the public mind, came into existence only at the beginning of the eighteenth century. We do not know for sure what kind of horse Celia rode, it is one of the many tantalising omissions from her journal. It is probable that she rode an Arab, a Barb imported from the Iberian peninsula, a native breed or a cross. As mentioned earlier, the horse which I rode is a cross between a thoroughbred and a Welsh Cob, a native breed. The Welsh Cob has an infusion of Arab and Andalusian blood, which in turn contains Barb blood. This ancestry dates probably from Roman times, and this gives the breed both stamina and quality. It is accepted that the Arab horse is outstanding for its speed and endurance and the native breeds for their stamina and their ability to exist on a basic diet.

Today the stables at Wandlebury have been turned into cottages and the area is a delightful place in which to live. The public, with their horses, are allowed into the area of the fort itself. The Via Devana is an interesting route: for much of its length it is a typical Roman road, built on a high agger, in places thirty five feet wide, with the land falling away on both sides. It is partly hedged, partly open, with a wide variety of trees, shrubs and flowers. It also afforded me some excellent views across open country to the south and, on the good going, opportunities for some steady canters. At the end of this stretch we came to the outskirts of Cambridge.

HORSES AND VEHICLES

From Loggan's *Oxonia Illustrata*

4

Cambridge to Stilton

Celia has a fair amount to say about Cambridge. Not surprisingly she enthuses about King's College Chapel but she also mentions Trinity College, the old Library, St John's, Queens', Clare and St Catharine's, then newly built and the chapel still unfinished. I could not of course ride round the colleges so I left Cameron behind and sought to follow Celia's route on foot. The magic of Cambridge which she enjoyed was still very much evident three hundred years later. To find the fountain in the quadrangle of Trinity, for instance, just as she found it was exciting and the feeling of tranquillity within the chapel, already two hundred years old when she saw it, was quite tangible. Her description of King's College Chapel as "... the finest building I have heard of; curious Carvings of Stone on the outside, twelve large windows and two at each end very large, all finely painted all over with the history of the New Testament ..." still holds good today, even though our world is immeasurably larger than hers and thousands of fine buildings have gone up since her time.

Undergraduates would then have ridden around on horses, some hired and some their own, but today the horses have been replaced by bicycles which crowd the streets. The streets are also crowded with tourists from all over the world and this too would seem strange to her eyes were she to return by some magic.

She also mentions the Backs, although she does not use that term. It may be that it came into use following the implementation of the plans drawn up by Capability Brown "...the river runs at the back side of most of the Colleges; they have fine stone bridges over it and gates that lead to fine walks". Today his design has come to be accepted as one of the most successful pieces of landscaping in the country.

It is interesting to compare her comments on Cambridge with those on Oxford, where she also wrote at some length on the colleges, other buildings, gardens and fine wide streets, ''well pitched''. She had connections with Oxford and it could be that she favoured it over Cambridge - perhaps she did not care for the narrow streets there. The two cities had then, as now, a quite different aspect. Perhaps we can trace here the rivalry between the two places which was familiar to children a couple of decades or more ago. Towards boat race time coloured favours would be worn and those who did not sport them would be asked which crew they supported. There was a curious undercurrent that it was right and proper to support Cambridge. I have been told of a conversation at school in the thirties in which two boys were discussing a third. He was agreed to be a strange kind of person: "he supports Oxford" said one of the boys as evidence of this fact.

The botanical garden in Cambridge was established later, after Celia's time, than the Oxford physic garden which she describes in some detail. She writes about the college gardens in both places. In Trinity College the garden was laid out in chequerboard plots and later an apple tree was planted there from the same stock as the one from Isaac Newton's home at Woolsthorpe Manor near Grantham, of which more later when we reach Lincolnshire. Reverting to Celia's attitude to the universities and to the whole subject of learning, we know little of her background and she may well have had little knowledge of or interest in academic matters. One has to remember that educated women were few and far between. The significance of the apple falling from the tree would probably have been lost on her. The proper education of women was to begin well after her time.

She makes no reference to the fairs at Cambridge which Defoe was to comment on twenty or more years later. He refers to the Sturbridge Fair; if the corn was not off the fields by a certain day in August, the stallholders moved in and simply trampled the crops. They had many booths or tents, placed in rows like streets, one being called Cheapside, which would cover all sorts of trades and would sell retail to people who had come mainly from London. The stallholders would be generally goldsmiths, turners, hatters, sellers of china, drapers and coffee shop proprietors, together with other purveyors of food and drink. There would be another row, mainly of larger booths, which would be for wholesalers. Here they would have ample room to bring in their packs and waggons to load and unload. Wholesale grocers would be there too, together with wine merchants and salters.

Packhorse trains would converge there from the north of England, bringing with them vast quantities of cloths, cottons, upholsterers' ware, blankets and rugs and woollen materials. Hops would also come in from the south to be traded and sent on to the breweries of the north. As many as fifty hackney coaches might be employed in transporting people to and from Cambridge. The last day of the fair would be the horse fair, where there would be horse and foot races as well as trading. The fair had to be completed by a certain day in September, otherwise the ploughmen would come straight in, with as little ceremony as the stallholders at the beginning, and overthrow all, and trample it into the dirt. The farmers charged the stallholders fees and one has to think of the occasional loss of crops in that context. All this was missed by Celia because she was there in the spring and not in August or September.

Today the magic of the place comes through and the modern traveller still has the impression of a city with a style of its own. It is, as with Norwich, a city which is always a joy to visit. The centre in both places is well preserved and Celia, miraculously transported forward in time to the twentieth century, would have no great difficulty in recognising where she is.

MEASURED from HICKS'S HALL.

LONDON TO CARLISLE, CONTINUED TO GLASGOW.

THRO' STAMFORD, NEWARK, DONCASTER, BOROUGHBRIDGE, APPLEBY, and MOFFAT.

EATON SOCON. Bushmead Priory, Rev. *Hugh Wade Gery.*

LITTLE PAXTON, 1 m. beyond, at Southoe, The Rectory, Rev. *Robert Pointer.*

ALCONBURY, before, Alconbury Lodge, *J. Newton*, Esq.

STILTON, 1½ m. distant, Washingley Hall, ———.

STILTON has long been celebrated for the excellence of its cheese, which not unfrequently has been called the English Parmesan: it is asserted that this article was first made by a Mrs. Paulet, of Wymondham, near Melton Mowbray, in Leicestershire, who supplied the celebrated Cooper Thornhill, who kept the Bell Inn in this village, with this new manufacture, which he often sold for 2*s.* 6*d.* per pound; and hence it is said to have received its name from the place of sale. This Thornhill was a famous rider, and is recorded to have won the cup at Kimbolton with a mare that he accidentally took on the course after a journey of 12 miles.

KATE'S CABIN INN, near, Alwalton Castle, *Buxton Kenrick*, Esq.

WANSFORD, 5 m. distant, Fineshade Abbey, Hon. *John Monkton.*

BRIDGE CASTERTON, 2 m. beyond, Tickencote Hall, *T. Fydell*, Esq.

HORN LANE TURNPIKE. Exton Hall, Sir *Gerard Noel Noel*, Bart. This mansion exhibits a fine specimen of that style of architecture which prevailed in the latter part of the 16th century, notwithstanding the great damage it received by a destructive fire that took place on the 24th May 1810, and which totally consumed one half of the south-east wing. The apartments are commodious, but some of them possess rather a gloomy appearance. The park and grounds are of immense extent, and contain an

From Glasgow		From London
	Beyond Buckden,	
	To Brampton Cross 2½ m., thence to Hinchinbroke 1 m. thence to Huntingdon ¾ m.	
	London to	
	* *HUNTINGDON, 65¼ m.*	
333	Brampton Hut	63½
	To Huntingdon 3 m.	
	to Thrapston 12½ m.	
330½	Alconbury	66
329¾	Alconbury Weston	66¾
328¾	* Alconbury Hill, *Wheatsheaf*	67¾
	To Huntingdon 5¼ m., thence to London, by Royston and Ware, 58¾ m.	
325¼	Sawtry St. Andrews	71¼
321½	* Stilton	75
320¾	Norman Cross	75¾
	To Peterborough 5¾ m.	
317¼	Kate's Cabin Inn	79¼
	To Peterborough 5 m.	
	to Oundle 8 m.	
315½	Water Newton	81
314¾	Sibson	81¾
313	* Wansford, *Turnpike*	83½
	to Oundle 9 m.	
	Cross the river Nen, and enter Northamptonshire.	
	To Peterborough 7¾ m.	
	to Uppingham 14 m.	
312¼	White Water Turnpike, *Northamptonshire*	84¼
	Entrance of Stamford,	
	To Kettering 22¾ m.	
	Cross the river Welland	

manor was granted to the see of Lincoln in the time of Henry I. by the abbot of Ely, as a compensation for the privilege of making his abbacy into a bishopric. Several of the prelates belonging to this see have been interred in the parish church, which is a very handsome structure, and contains monumental erections to their memory, that will by many be considered worthy of examination.——Beyond Buckden, in the road to Huntingdon, Hinchinbroke House, Countess of *Sandwich*; Brampton Park, Lady *Olivia Sparrow*; The Views, *John Maule*, Esq.; and Rev. — *Walker.*

SAWTRY ST. ANDREWS, 1 m. beyond, Connington Castle, *John Heathcote*, Esq.; and 2 m. farther, Holme Wood, Capt. *Wells.*

KATE'S CABIN INN, 2 m. distant, at Overton Longville, Earl of *Aboyne*; and on the opposite bank of the river Nen, Milton Park, Earl *Fitzwilliam.*

WHITE WATER TURNPIKE, 1 m. before, Walcot Hall, *unoccupied*; and Ufford Hall, *unoccupied.*

STAMFORD, 1 m. before, Burleigh House, Marquis of *Exeter;* near which is Wothorp, or Worthorp House, a dilapidated structure, belonging to the same nobleman.

BRIDGE CASTERTON, 1½ m. distant, Tolethorpe House, *E. Harrison*, Esq.

BRIDGE CASTERTON. This place, which is situated on the Roman Ermine Street, has caused more difference of opinion among antiquaries, than perhaps any other spot in the British empire: some affirm it to be the Gausennæ, or Causennis, which others place at Nottingham; and many suppose that it is the Durobrivis of the Itinerary; others again believe that its present name has given an appellation to Kesteven, in Lincolnshire, and nearly all of them in fact differ either with respect

From Cambridge to Huntingdon Celia took a route via Fenstanton which means that she probably travelled along the Roman road which the modern A604 uses. I rode on a southerly route as far as Bourn, using the newly created Wimpole Way which is a route from Cambridge to the National Trust property of Wimpole Hall for walkers, riders and cyclists.

We had to cross the M11 by bridge again - as one approaches the bridge one's heart is always in one's mouth knowing that Cameron has little experience of such hazards. However, it was Sunday and the road was quieter than on the occasion of our previous crossing but we went over at a smart trot just the same. It was with a great sense of relief that I rode on through the village of Coton, where I noted with some amusement the sign on the village green which read ''no horses''. I know only too well that horses can churn up a green in wet weather but greens were meeting places and for feeding animals and were not intended to look like suburban gardens. How I hate the country being made to look like the town and one is aware of this ''plague'' everywhere. It is interesting to note, by the way, that the ancient ridge path along which I was travelling has many parish boundaries aligned along it, although there are some modern deviations.

I enjoyed the warm sunshine, Cameron going steadily at a walk, trot or occasional canter. We had a couple of slight alarms near Harwick Wood. The track was very narrow in places, with deep ditches on both sides and Cameron, with his big feet, would slip the odd hind foot off here and there. The danger is that when one foot goes, the rest of the horse can so easily follow. A few yards farther and I found to my dismay that most of a narrow plank bridge was missing; I slid off Cameron's back, keeping my arm firmly round his neck to save me from falling into the deep ditch. He then walked behind me over the remaining plank, displaying his usual trust in me. I had to lead him for some little way as there was no possibility of remounting at that point. We then carried on without further hazard, following the well defined portway to Caxton.

At the time of Celia's ride many changes were taking place. In what was to be termed by W G Hoskins ''The Great Rebuilding'' many of the large substantial timber-framed medieval farmhouses had floors inserted to provide living rooms and bedrooms. The most common type consisted of three ground rooms, kitchen, living room and parlour, with bedrooms above. Later the fronts were bricked up and the thatch removed. It was also a time of great cottage building: these cottages consisted typically of only two ground floor rooms with a single central chimney between them. By the end of the seventeenth century there was an increasing use of brick and tile as well as chalk blocks and clay, and the chimney stack tended to be put on externally.

Celia would also have noticed the flooding of water meadows in winter to produce early pasture for sheep which was frost free when drained. It was also a method of fertilisation, the land gaining from nutrients in the water, and the layout of these water meadows can still be seen today as one rides across country.

Caxton was an important stopping place in coaching times and is on Ermine Street which we rode along through a number of counties in the course of our journey. There is a grim reminder of the harshness of past times in the gibbet which marks the place where three men were once hanged for sheep stealing and are buried close by.

We took the route to Eltisley along a lovely lane. Although the going was heavy and at times we had to criss-cross the deep ruts made by farm machinery, taking care that Cameron didn't stumble, the obviously ancient route with its hedges and ditches on both sides made for enjoyable riding. However I had to proceed at a walk for much of the time.

Eltisley is a pleasant village with houses surrounding a large green close to the busy A45. I had to wait many minutes for a gap in the fast moving traffic to cross this road as my route took me northwards. It was one of those occcasions when a backup is invaluable and my husband was able to undertake the chore of opening and closing gates and enabling me to stand well back from the traffic until the way was clear. This gave me one less thing to worry about. Even with a gap in the traffic it is never pleasant to cross busy roads like the A45, there is always the danger that a horse will stop half way across and refuse to carry on. However, safely across with no incidents, we followed the bridleways via Yelling and Graveley into Godmanchester. Although the countryside was open and fairly flat it was by no means without interest. One could see for miles and all the tracks were open, except for one near Graveley which was very wet and difficult to negotiate.

Quaker Meeting Place, Godmanchester

At one part water was lying to some depth, at least up to Cameron's girth. We had to resort to scrambling up a high bank with me clinging to his mane and then following the field edge round. As we approached Godmanchester we were on high wide open land with a few scattered farmsteads and the atmosphere was that of Cold Comfort Farm. We had travelled another twenty five miles towards our goal. It is said that Celia Fiennes' estimates of mileage are unreliable. One has to remember, however, that she would have had to make deviations, as indeed one has to sometimes today, and also that in the south she was using the statute mile while in the north she was using the old English mile. Hours in the saddle is a better yardstick, in the same way that signposts in the Swiss Alps and other mountainous areas refer, sensibly, to so many hours' walking.

In the late afternoon we reached Godmanchester which, in the sixteenth and seventeenth centuries and earlier, was a rival town to Huntingdon. One can understand the problems which Celia encountered with the "fenny ways". Watery ways abound in this whole area. Godmanchester is an attractive place, with weirs and boating now, but also with some seventeenth century architecture still evident. The only way now for horse riders to cross into Huntingdon is under the modern A604 road from Cambridge to the A1 Great North Road. Heavy traffic abounds on all these roads. The centre of Huntingdon has only two remaining churches of the sixteen, together with four monasteries and two hospitals, which existed here in the Middle Ages. When the Civil War began there were four churches. Part of the old Grammar School which Cromwell attended is still there as a Cromwellian museum. The building dates back to Norman times and was at one stage a hospital in the sense of a resting place for travellers, from which the word hospitality is of course derived. Although plasticky shopfronts abound, one can still trace the seventeenth century street plan and, with a little imagination, the market stalls, pedlars and travellers can be visualised in the area around the parish church. Huntingdon grew briefly in importance with the growth of river navigation and as a key posting house. The George Inn is still there with, in the yard, the old layout with open balconies visible. Travellers could rent suites of rooms to carry on their business or to rest. There is a strong sense of history here as it was the Falcon Inn, with its bowed oriel window above the arch, which Cromwell made his Civil War headquarters. A notice is still there, proclaiming that he wanted good Christians and not Quakers or dissenters.

I visited Hinchingbrook House, Cromwell's birthplace, which is now a school but is open to the public on Sundays. However, I was not able to go into the house which Celia describes in great detail. It had great lofty rooms and many fine hangings, good pictures and furniture. The gardens, at the time she visited, were unfinished and were being laid out with dwarf trees and gravel walks, a wilderness and a greenhouse (a very early mention). I managed a brief walk round the garden and surveyed the view southwards from the terrace which Celia describes. She speaks of the country being fruitful and much like Oxfordshire. It is no surprise that Celia stayed here as her father was, of course, a colonel in Cromwell's army.

The Old River Bridge in Huntingdon was built in 1332 to carry Ermine Street over the Ouse. It has six arches and was considered to be one of the finest in England. It was built from both ends simultaneously by two different authorities but without much regard for direction. The two parts met in the middle but on different axes and there is a bend which has to be negotiated. Pepys had a house nearby which is still there but is in private ownership.

I left the network of modern roads around Huntingdon and rode north. The weather had changed; the morning had started cold and very wet and in few minutes I was soaked. Cameron was not liking the rain and was jumping around, ducking his head this way and that. He was full of himself for the first few miles so whenever possible we trotted on both to keep us warm and also to prevent him from spooking at imaginary dangers at every turn.

Route planning on this section was difficult as there are three possible routes. Two are medieval or earlier and there is a more modern route consisting largely of bridleways and quiet enclosure lanes to the west. I opted for the Bullock Road which is believed to be pre-medieval. Travellers would leave the Roman road at Alconbury Hill and at Alconbury there are the remains of an ancient bridge.

Close to the main road we began this leg of our journey just as the travellers in past centuries would have done. I found myself in delightful scenery of little woods and hills and left the village of Alconbury. On the first bridleway after Alconbury which I tried I found that the line was undefined and I used the roads until I got to Upton. I was delighted to find a wide lane looking just as it must have done when the drovers and other travellers were using it. In places it was deeply rutted, caused by farm machinery going back and forth.

This route took me through to Glatton, with the way bounded for the most part by two ditches and in quite a few places by hedges as well. As I rode the ditches abounded with cowslips and in the woodland bluebells were just coming out. I felt sure that this was the route which Celia took, as Ermine Street had fallen into disuse and she rode in sight of the "great water" of Whittlesey Mere. She described it as "looking like some sea, it being so high and of a great length. This is part of the fenny country. It is three mile broad and six mile long, in the midst is a little island where a great store of wild fowl breeds, there is no coming near it in a mile or two, the ground is all wet and marshy but there are several little channels runs into it which by boats people go up to this place; when you enter the mouth of the mere it looks formidable and is often very dangerous by reason of sudden winds that will rise like hurricanes in the mere, but at other times people boat it around the mere with pleasure; there is an abundance of good fish in it this was thought to have been the sea some time ago, and all choked up so remains all about it for some miles a fenny marsh ground for those little rivers that runs to the sea.''

Now it has been drained and is in agricultural use but one can still trace some of the original farmsteads. It covered 1570 acres when a detailed map was produced in the 1780s. The Mere was used for fishing and wildfowling. In the winter ice skating was popular and in the summer it was frequented by ``parties of pleasure''. It was the yachtsmen who were opposed to the draining of the Mere as amongst those who made their living from it. The reclamation started in 1853 and there is a farm called Engine Farm, from the site of one of the great beam engines which were an essential part of the nineteenth century fenland landscape. The appearance of the Mere today is just as other drained fens but one can imagine the skating in winter and the boating parties in summer, people travelling there no doubt in their carriages or on horseback. But then there is often a feeling of sadness about reclaimed land. In The Netherlands one can sometimes see an image of a fish or a ship on a wall, serving as a reminder of how drastically the landscape has changed.

I noted on the road that there are still one or two ponds left which are no doubt used for watering. The names of places along the route such as Coldharbour Farm, Cowpasture Farm and Moonshine Gap remind us that cattle would have been pastured there on the way to London while Flittermere Farm and Washingley would have been watering places. W G Hoskins has traced the continuation of the route we were using up to the River Trent at Newark, along the boundary between Leicestershire and Lincolnshire, so I looked forward to joining it again later.

At Caldecote there is a deserted village and the road and houses can still be traced but the people left in the Middle Ages and so Celia would have seen it as we did. I had no time for further exploration and went on into Stilton.

5

Stilton to Leicester

Stilton is, of course, famous for the cheese which was sold and originally made there. However, its production had ceased by Celia's time. The appearance of the place had changed drastically in the three hundred years which have elapsed. There would then have been a vast amount of traffic up and down the Great North Road - carriages, ridden horses, pack ponies, postboys and driven herds of cattle and flocks of geese. Indeed, as recently as 150 years ago oxen were being shod in the place and there was stabling for over three hundred horses at one time in The Angel. All this bustle of activity would have called for a large number of people employed in various establishments along the main street.

I found the Bell Inn, newly built when Celia rode through, falling into decay and the whole atmosphere of the place was of somewhere where things used to happen, rather like a deserted western town in a film. The enclosures took place in that area not long after Celia's time and it is of interest to note that the enclosure commissioners held their meetings at The Bell or at The Angel, the other coaching inn across the road. I purchased some Stilton in a small supermarket, in itself a sign of change, and there was a pervading feeling of change in the air. The cheese was ready cut, plastic wrapped and not made locally. In the post office and store a customer was in conversation with the proprietor as I entered. She was bemoaning the fact that houses were going to be built in the village and that its character would change as a result. "It happened at Sawtry" (nearby) she said "and that's why I left there." "There used to be a wheelwright and carpenter here" echoed the proprietor "until quite recent times." "Where was that?" asked the customer. "Why, in the yard just behind here" he replied.

On her way north from Stilton, Celia described a cross that directed three ways - to York, London and Oatly. The last named was probably Oatley, a village near Ellesmere in Shropshire and the site of an Elizabethan mansion. It seems curious that such a small place should merit mention on a signpost a hundred or more miles distant, but Ellesmere stands at the junction of two routes into Wales, one via Oswestry and one via Wrexham. I took time to find out whether this cross still existed but drew a blank. What I did discover, however, was a large signpost in stone on the central reservation of the A1 at Alconbury.

It was not easy to reach. To have attempted it on horseback would have been insane, and even on foot one had to wait for a break in the fast, roaring traffic and then run. What I found was a signpost erected after Celia's time by the Turnpike Trust and pointing to London by two stagecoach routes, one via Cambridge and one via Biggleswade and Hatfield. It is in fact illustrated in "The Old Roads of England" by Sir William Addison.

I travelled on from Stilton but on the next section problems began. The track started wide enough but there were horses in the adjacent field galloping up and down and this "set Cameron alight". His head shot up with excitement, and he snorted and started to float along at a trot, always a danger signal with him. All I could do was to sit quietly and pull him up to a walk. Once safely past, the silly horse spooked at a tree stump and, much to my embarrassment, shied into the wheat field leaving his large hoofprints in the growing crops. Then at the next gateway the track petered out and we had no alternative other than to navigate across a field of young wheat. However, we came out at about the right place and followed the track towards the road. Just before we turned onto the road a tractor and sprayer swung into our path and stopped just short of us. Cameron was, not surprisingly, somewhat het up and we bounced over the tractor's bumper into the road, luckily with both of us in one piece. I reflected on how stupid some people can be.

We turned off the road at Ongutein Manor Farm and on my way down to the Billing Brook found that the tractor was following me. If I slowed the driver slowed, if I trotted faster he speeded up. I stopped by some derelict buildings to let him past and he turned in. So I called out to him "Which way are you going?" so that I could keep out of his way. His response was, to my surprise, "I am following you round the farm". One has to be determined and to know one's rights to use rights of way today: there are problems which Celia knew nothing of. The man's manner then softened and he asked me where I was going and hazarded that I was not local. I told him that I had ridden from north of London and was heading north, navigating across country with the aid of my map. He told me that the brook at the bottom had lost its bridge because of flooding and in places the bottom was very soft. I rode to the river, dismounted, scrambled down to the water's edge and pushed my whip into the water. The river appeared to be deep and with no hard bottom. I decided that it was not safe to attempt a crossing, especially as the line of the bridleway was not clearly defined on the other side. There should have been another bridleway at that point but I could detect no sign of it. This was the first serious obstacle which we had met in our journey. I was forced to backtrack to the nearest road and try another way round. Cameron loves exploring new territory and he hates backtracking; his ears go back, his head goes down and he sulks for some while. This is just what he did on this occasion but he just has to learn to take the rough with the smooth.

Christopher Taylor, in his book "Roads & Tracks of Britain", says ''The farm with the odd name of Ongutein Manor. This has great significance because just below the farm there was, until wantonly destroyed without warning, a small moated site. It was little more than a square island, surrounded by a broad water-filled ditch, but it was the site of a medieval house called Ogerston. The importance of this apparently minor place is that it is actually marked on the Great Gough Map of England and Wales, made in 1360. As all places on that map appear to lie on main roads, the existence of Ogerston shows that at that period the lane which passes it today was the main road to the north. As it also went through the main street of Coppingford and Upton, which had probably existed in that form for three centuries, we are able to establish a period of long usage of this route.''

Today Cameron kept picking up sharp stones and ended the day with slightly bruised feet: the thoroughbred in him gives him thin soles, unfortunately. But no harm was done and he was to suffer no ill effects the following morning. Both of us finished the day cold, wet and fed up, knowing that it meant an unnecessary section of roadwork to rejoin the next bridleway. The ray of light at the end of the tunnel was that my husband realised that we must be lost or stuck and so returned with the trailer to find us and give us a lift to the night's stabling.

The next day, all these problems behind us, I set off in lovely sunshine and with high hopes of no further bridleway difficulties. I rode north-east to the village of Warmington to join a bridleway from the busy A605 Oundle-Peterborough road. For reasons of safety I led Cameron down the road until I had negotiated a gate south of Elton Park. I climbed onto the bank to remount, Cameron is a big horse to get on, and as I rode on I noted signs of ridge and furrow, so it seemed likely that this land had been emparked following its earlier cultivation by the villagers. Through the woodland we had lovely glimpses of the River Nene, just beyond which, but out of sight, was Fotheringay Castle where Mary Queen of Scots was imprisoned. It is interesting that Fotheringay church was not built until the fifteenth century, at a time when practically all other church building in the Midlands had ceased.

I was pleased to see the bridleway signed and waymarked and we entered Elton Park, having had the hassle of opening and closing as many as five gates. My reward, however, was to find myself in a beautiful park. The hall, which has evolved over many centuries, is a fascinating building. The Elizabethan part was mainly pulled down just before Celia's ride and rebuilt and it has been added to over the last three hundred years. The gardens have been much simplified in this time and the topiary and formal gardens have in the main been removed. It was disappointing that I had only a distant view of this impressive hall. It seems certain that this was the place noted by Celia on her way to Wansford from Stilton. She described it as "a Gentlemans house that stands finely on a hill in a parke pretty high with fine groves about it".

Here I found the recurring difficulty of negotiating open tracts of land in unfamiliar countryside. Having discovered that I had taken a wrong bearing I decided that the way ahead was to backtrack and go through yet another gate and over a tributary of the Nene which forms the county boundary. However, there was a mass of mud and mire which had first to be crossed and which turned out to be over Cameron's knees. I had a further problem here in that he hesitated and refused to go forward and I had to dismount. Once I reached the gate, which was closed with a barbed wire tie and with barbed wire wrapped round the gatepost, I realised I could not have opened it from horseback anyway. I had to heave it open but as we floundered through the miry section I caught myself and my saddle on the barbed wire. This nearly made me fall. With Cameron plunging alongside me the situation was potentially dangerous and I had to find a way to extricate myself from it as quickly as possible. Safely across, my first task was to find somewhere to tie Cameron up while I struggled back across the mire to fasten the gate. Having done this I realised that I was in a filthy state but luckily the weather was warm and I was drying out quickly. I led Cameron for a short distance as he was het up with all the recent excitement and with so many sheep around - he was brought up with pigs from foalhood but sheep he does find intimidating.

But my problems were still not over. Every time I went to remount, he kept jumping about. This was unlike him as he has always been taught to stand and not to move when I am trying to mount. So I continued to lead him for a while while I looked for a suitable mounting block. But he suddenly jumped sideways, taking me in his path, knocking me to the ground and then going

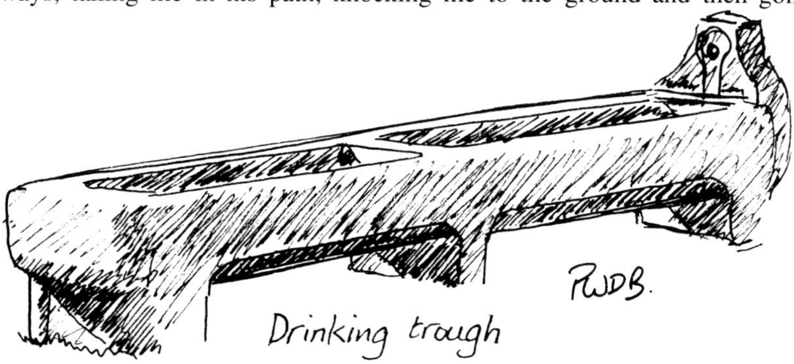

Drinking trough

down himself. In those few moments I really wondered if my ride was over. As I started to collect my wits I found to my horror that Cameron was free as in the confusion I had lost my reins. It crossed my mind that I might be quite unable to catch him, loose in a large park with plenty of grass. If I had not been so badly shaken up I should have remembered a passage from a book by the famous rider Tschiffely "... as soon as an animal comes to a region which is strange to him he will never go away from his master but will look for his company and in case of danger seek his protection..." How true that is: I offered Cameron a Polo mint, he immediately came to me and I was able to remount from a nearby fallen tree. It was an altogether nasty episode from which I had emerged in one piece although very badly bruised. At such times one really wonders why one rides across country exploring unfamiliar areas.

I spent most of that evening and that night soaking my bruises in witch hazel and I was very stiff for the next few days. Later I went to hospital for an X-ray and felt discomfort for some weeks, but that's one of the hazards of long-distance riding. Fortunately, nothing was broken. The doctor at the hospital offered me a sling for my arm but this I rejected as I could not have continued to ride with such a handicap.

Feeling sore and angry about my fall, I rode on the the next track, close to the River Nene. This track was open, waymarked and easy to follow from my Ordnance Survey map. We paused for a break and I let Cameron have some grass. Another rider approached, stopped for a chat and I told her of my adventures in Elton Park. She had not ridden that far from home and did not know the area. Her comment, on seeing my appearance, was that she thought I had fallen off into deep mud. So on yet another day I ended up filthy. At least with modern garments one can normally manage to dry wet clothes overnight or, on sunny days, they will dry on you. Celia would have had a problem with her heavy garments if her long rides had not taken place during hot, dry summers.

Shortly we arrived at Wansford where we crossed over the bridge which Celia Fiennes probably crossed. It is a well cared for village which must have changed somewhat since she was there. She remarks "as I pass'd the road I saw upon the walls of ordinary peoples houses and walls of their outhouses the cow dung plaister'd up to drie in cakes which they used for firing - its a very offensive fewell but country people use little else in these parts". None was in evidence in the twentieth century. The bridge at Wansford is at the joining of three counties: Northamptonshire, Lincolnshire and the old county of Rutland, now part of Leicestershire. Celia stayed at The Swan and she tells of Wansford being called Wanstead-in-England, arising from the story of "a man makeing hay fell asleep on a heap of it and a great storme washed the hay and man into the River, and carry'd him to the Bridge, where he awoke and knew not where he was, called to the people in the grounds and told them he liv'd in a place called Wanstead in England, which goes for a jest on the men of Wanstead (Wansford) to this day''. The Swan is still there and indeed carries a huge painting of the incident on its front wall. I passed close to Thorpe Hall on my way out of Wansford, a house mentioned by Celia Fiennes. It stands on a hill in a fine park but I could see little of the house because of the many trees which had grown up around it.

Leicester Meeting House

And on to Duddington. As Celia had before me, I passed over the very good stone bridge, noting in the parapet an unusual parish boundary marker. Close by was a mill with water rushing down the race, something which was not mentioned by Celia but probably seen by her. The houses and walls in this district are built of local stone and I had noted several quarries in the course of our travels, commented on by Celia.

I was at this point close to the Leicestershire border, so it occurred to me to question why I should go directly to Stamford. It seemed sense rather to make a diversion of several days to take in Leicester and the battlefield of Market Bosworth; also I would be able to ride to Leicester by means of the Gartree Road, the continuation of the Via Devana in Cambridgeshire. So I crossed the county boundary into Leicestershire, a county unfamiliar to me. A change of scenery was immediately apparent as we climbed the hills and I enjoyed the expansive views and noted much evidence of ridge and furrow, which indicated that the land had never been under cultivation since before the enclosures. It was sheep and cattle country and well defined woods, part of the old Rockingham Forest, completed the altogether pleasing scene.

When I reached the farmhouse where we were to spend the night, another peculiarity of the Leicestershire scene became apparent. There were some oddities about the construction of the house and upon enquiry it emerged that it had been a pub. Apparently it is quite common for a pub and a farm to be run as one enterprise in this part of the country. As the agriculture is largely concerned with stock and is not arable, harvest time does not pose a problem and the practice is good economics, albeit hard work. Another feature of the local scene was an interest in historic tractors. Our host had several in everyday use and as I set off to the next village for dinner I met yet another one in the lane.

Celia had also noted the special character of Leicestershire with its ''red land, good corne of all sorts and grass both fields and inclosures; you see a great way upon their hills the bottoms full of enclosures woods and different sorts of manuring and herbage, amongst which are placed many little towns, which gives great pleasure to travellers to view; the miles are long but hitherto pretty hard good way to Coppingham (Uppingham) 5 miles more, which is a neate market town; Satturday is their market which is very good affording great quantetys of corn leather yarne and cattle, such a concourse of people that my landlord told me he used to have 100 horse set up at his inn, and there were many publick houses here; and you see very large fine sheep and very good land but very deep bad roads; from hence to Leister which they call but 13 mile but the longest 16 I ever went and the most tiresome, being full of sloughs, clay deep way, that I ever was neer 11 hours going but 25 mile - as they reckoned it - between Wansford and Leicester town, a footman could have gone much faster than I could ride''. Originally, of course, a footman did not wait at table or ride on a carriage but would run ahead of the master or mistress when they rode on horseback and a fleet footman was much prized. Celia was, by the way, using the long mile and not the statute mile in the above extract.

I continued my ride, taking a southern route, covering several miles cross-country on good tracks through a large park now under cultivation. How lucky I was, it was another warm day and both Cameron and I were enjoying ourselves. In the distance I could see an inviting plantation and, looking at my map, noticed that the bridleway went through it to the next village. On nearing the plantation I found that the track disappeared and we followed the line of a hedge, watching out for rabbit holes, until we reached a sleeper bridge. But, to my horror, I then discovered that some of the sleepers were missing. I dismounted to see if we could dare risk it across what was left of the bridge but, on examination, I found that the whole structure was unsound. I wandered around the edge of the plantation, leading Cameron and looking for an alternative route, but eventually gave up and decided that I had to backtrack for about four miles and go round by the metalled road. It was now getting quite late in the afternoon and I had visions of reaching our night's stop uncomfortably late.

When one has to backtrack continually one can nearly double one's daily mileage and it is difficult to convey adequately just how depressing such a waste of effort on a cross-country journey can be. Leicestershire is a hunting county with a high level of horse ownership: it seemed incongruous to find the bridleways to be well signposted and waymarked but obviously little used and with gaps such as the damaged bridge which no one had bothered to get put right. The point has to be appreciated that these blockages of bridleways are quite simply blockages of the Queen's highway. Would blockages of the metalled road be tolerated with the same apparent complacency? It is nothing short of a national scandal that the authorities allow such conditions to exist. Also there were various old railway routes which, sadly, had not been put to recreational use, but this is hardly surprising in view of the lack of attention being paid to existing routes.

Riding across Leicestershire I encountered worse conditions from any other part of the country in which I had yet been. I found myself caught up in a recurring pattern of trying to navigate along undefined ways, with many fords or bridges to cross, gates on narrow bridges requiring one to dismount, double gates like cattle crushes with no room to turn the horse and, worst of all, gates with a piece of wire stretched across them about a foot above the ground which had to be unhooked and rehooked. Often, one even had to climb over the gate just in order to unhook the wire. Through all these hazards there were many sheep and bullocks to contend with as well. One had, however, to set against these difficulties the glorious scenery and the sense of wide open space all around.

But fortunately things did begin to improve. The bridleway through to the one-time village of Nevill Holt was clear, the only real difficulty was the fact that the gates along the route were not designed to be operated from horseback. There was another problem, although blame could not be laid at anyone's door for it, in that in one field Cameron and I were suddenly surrounded by a herd of inquisitive bullocks. Cameron tensed up as he was fresh and I did wonder if he might buck me off. However, I decided to anticipate his possible reaction and dismounted, leading him through the herd and flicking my whip at the beasts to keep them at bay. Eventually I was safely past but I still had the recurring problem of remounting. Yet again I climbed onto the nearest gate and got into the saddle from there. However, I was rewarded for my efforts by the view of Nevill Holt on the hilltop above us, with the Hall and church spire standing up among the trees of the old parkland. That is all that is left of a one-time village which decayed after the open fields were enclosed. The Hall is a splendid medieval house of many periods dating from the fifteenth century, with Hall Farm remaining virtually unaltered from the late seventeenth century. Once past the Hall my reward was even greater as I rode towards the Welland Valley and the view unfolded before me almost as though I were in an aircraft. Cameron walked down the steep hill with commendable steadiness and into the village of Medbourne.

The Roman Gartree Road passes through Medbourne, a large attractive village which has been inhabited since Roman times. It has always been prosperous, as evidenced by the number of interesting houses both large and small. The Manor House, behind its seventeenth century facade, is a remarkable survival of a late thirteenth century house, and the Old Hall is a house with two cross wings dating from the mid-seventeenth century. The village kept its open fields in cultivation as late as 1844 and was much praised by Thoresby, the diarist and traveller, for its husbandry and productivity when he visited in 1790. Where the Roman road passes through the village there is a delightful four-arch medieval packhorse bridge which was restored at the time of our Queen's jubilee.

Having left Medbourne, we joined the Gartree Road at Glooston. This road probably went from Ermine Street at Alconbury Hill through to Leicester and could well have been a part of the Via Devana. The Medbourne-Glooston stretch of the road cannot, however, be ridden. But the mere fact of finding this old road still intact gave me that sense of the continuity of history which rewards the traveller from time to time. And to be able to ride for a number of miles with no navigational problems, other than opening and closing gates and crossing fords, was pleasure indeed. It was on this stretch that I came upon an old signpost which said "Leicester 13". It is likely that when this signpost was erected this route was in common use by all forms of traffic.

As I neared the next village of Carlton Curlieu the weather changed very quickly and we were soon in the midst of heavy driving rain with claps of thunder. Under these conditions one gets soaked through in a few minutes and Cameron jiggled sideways in an attempt to avoid the rain. At this point a big dog fox crossed our path and disappeared into a nearby field: one seldom sees them during the day at this time of the year. For some reason this triggered another quite different thought and I recalled that I had read that the inhabitants of Carlton Curlieu were, in the seventeenth century and earlier, noted for speaking in a peculiar manner. Burton said, in 1620, that "all those who are born here have a harsh and rattling kind of speech, uttering their words with great difficulty, and wharling in the throat, and cannot well pronounce the letter r". Later the same century Fuller attributed this "to some occult quality in the elements of the place" but it was probably due to the fact that the villagers were a Danish community of free peasants who had retained this peculiar way of speaking. By the late eighteenth century, however, it had apparently disappeared.

In view of the appalling weather conditions, it was just as well that we were nearing the closest point to Leicester to which I had intended to ride. Although soaked to the skin and almost shivering with cold I dismounted with a sense of satisfaction at having travelled along the very route which Celia had probably used. I was more than usually delighted to see my backup transport waiting at the appointed place. I quickly popped Cameron into the trailer, gave him water and a haynet and tried to dry him off a bit, took off my soaking wet anorak and then enjoyed a well deserved cup of coffee.

Leicester has been an important place since Roman times. The city had a Roman castle until just before Celia rode, it was dismantled in 1645 at the time of the Civil War. She liked Leicester, with its four gates and large well-pitched streets, and its market place and town hall. She saw a piece of the Jewry Wall which was 20 feet high and 70 feet long; it took its name from a ghetto and was composed of Roman bricks and rubble, being part of a Roman forum. Evelyn did not share her enthusiasm for the place, however. He described it as an old and ragged city, despicably built and later Baskerville reported it as an old and stinking town. Celia noted the existence of a piped water supply and, on a different point, the presence of a great many dissenters. This last observation may perhaps have coloured her judgment on the place as a whole. The tradition of religious dissent lives on. In Churchgate is the Great Meeting nonconformist chapel which dates back to 1708 and the main structure remains unaltered. The tradition of nonconformity is still a strong influence; indeed a twentieth century observer went on record that he found difficulty in obtaining good food and drink, and he was convinced that this was a hangover from the once held belief that good eating was synonymous with gluttony.

After Celia's time, Leicester was considerably expanded and over a thousand acres were enclosed for housing. The burgesses with pasture rights originally refused the enclosure of their fields and borough elections were fought on this issue. Candidates who wanted enclosure were burnt in effigy with their supporters wheeled about in muck carts. Eventually, after a long struggle, the land was enclosed and sold.

The famous breed of Leicester sheep was in evidence in Celia's time and Leicester was in the heart of the grazing district of the English plain. The sheep gave rise to a textile industry which has continued to be important into present times and it has been said that one can be completely clothed from head to toe with the products of the city.

Moving from the material world to the spiritual one, Cardinal Wolsey died there and Chaucer is said to have lived and married there. Also Wesley was a frequent visitor and the missionary Carey lived and worked there as a cobbler right up to the time he set off on his travels.

On getting up the following morning, I was still extremely stiff and sore after my fall and felt unable to cope with riding on to Market Bosworth. It would have been a difficult ride, with many changes of direction, a great deal of roadwork and many busy roads to negotiate. I decided therefore to take some time off and box Cameron to Stamford, then continue north as originally planned.

6

Travel in the Seventeenth Century

The countryside of seventeenth century England was not like it is today, with fields, hedgerows and streams. The land had yet to be criss-crossed with railways and the huge expansion of villages and towns, some into large conurbations, had yet to take place. It was a small nation with a population of about three million at the beginning of the century and five at its termination. Half or even more of the land was wilderness - heath, moor and common with a sparse population of squatters and here and there lean starving cattle of labouring folk. The rest of the countryside consisted of wide stretches of unfenced ploughlands, more than half of it worked on the old common field system from the long defunct feudal era.

Just before Celia's time the fields were encompassed by hedges and one could spend as long as half a day on a journey travelling between one hedge and the next or through a tree belt. Sparsely populated too were the water-logged and uncultivated fenlands. The country was indeed very different from the way that we know it today.

The expansion of industry and commerce was leading to increased traffic on the roads, no longer restricted to pilgrims, great landowners and the frequenters of fairs. The condition of the highways was deplorable in the extreme. The only roads with good foundations were those made by the Romans more than fourteen centuries earlier and the situation was made worse by the fact that wheeled traffic was beginning, the riding horse, packhorse and litter no longer sufficing. Up to that time the only wheeled vehicles were agricultural carts and those were few in number and in local use only. Strings of packhorses and droves of cattle were still using the roads and the state of them became at times near impossible, large teams of horses and oxen pulling carts serving to make the roads totally impassable in places.

Maintenance of the roads was the responsibility of the parishes, many of which were very poor and could by no means cope. Parishes in better off areas and especially where there were quarries of road-making materials were better placed. Where such materials were not to hand, sadly medieval monuments, shrines, monastic ruins and so on were used to supplement the usual materials of loose stones, pebbles, flint, chalk, lime, slag and cinders. The road surface was only roughly beaten down and any hard material available strewn on top.

The wheels of heavily laden carts though would create deep ruts and the surface would soon be destroyed. Bundles of heather or faggots were sometimes spread on the ridges in an attempt to improve matters. Mud from ditches was also thrown onto the roads but this in turn caused further problems.

In the Weald of Kent it was common practice to plough the roads at the onset of the better weather and lay the surface soil in a half circle to dry. Sometimes the highway consisted of narrow raised tracks with a quagmire on both sides onto which unfortunate riders had to venture when meeting waggons or strings of packhorses. The whole thing was a constant hindrance to travel in the neighbourhood of market towns. When the land was enclosed the roads frequently wore into hollow lanes which were so narrow that the wheels wore them into a diversity of tracks which were either deep, stony, rough, high or low according to the natural surface.

Each season of the year imparted a different character to the roads. In summer there was suffocating dust, something with which the early motorists would have to contend two centuries later, while spring and autumn became the rutting seasons, with deep ruts full of water and high ridges which could easily overturn a coach. In winter the mud levelled the road and ditch to one quagmire and ice and thaw brought their own peculiar dangers. Of all the dangers, however, floods were by far the most serious. Even summer showers would raise the water level sufficient to hinder traffic for hours and in winter it might even take days for a coach or waggon to complete its journey. Riders would sometimes forsake the roads altogether and take advantage of the higher ground to the side and canny landowners might make them pay for the privilege.

Oliver Heywood, the famous nonconformist preacher from near Halifax, provides a vivid description of an incident in 1680. He wrote ‘‘I met a man riding on a horse and driving two horses before him with pack saddles, yet empty. He had tied them together with a halter. Now just as I met him there was a deep hollow way below and a high causey above, and one of the horses took the higher, and the other the lower way. It was impossible that the lower should leap up to the other and there was great hazard of the higher falling, and both ways they could not go for the distance was beyond the reach of the halter .... At last the man, fearing the issue, light off his horses and run towards the lower horse to pull off the halter; but as he ran the horse in the hollow way leapt up with his forefeet to mount the causey, but was not able, fell down and pulled the other one backwards after him. With the fall was a crashing noise. I made account that the horse's back or neck had been broken, for he lay the horse with his feet upwards and stirred not .... However, there was no hurt except for two bakestones on the horse that fell which were masht to pieces and the man made a great lamentation for the breach of the Baking Stones.''

The sheer size of the amount of packhorse traffic has to be appreciated. Daniel Defoe states that a thousand horse packs were needed to convey cloth from Yorkshire and Lancashire to fairs in Cambridgeshire and carry hops back on the return journey. Packhorse trains of a similar size also carried lead ore from the mines to the smelting mills. The approach of a packhorse train was heralded by the sound of bells attached to the collar of the leading horse. This would warn approaching riders to get out of the way as the train could not stop, but what happened if two trains met is not recorded. On broader roads riders would find it difficult to keep to the track owing to the packhorse trains, whifflers (an official who cleared the way for a procession), women riding to market with large panniers and all manner of other traffic. This might well compel an approaching rider to cross the track as many as twenty times in one mile. In difficult country a guide might have to be employed for two or three shillings a day, plus his food, drink and lodgings. Boats were frequently used in winter for horses and riders although sometimes the horses would be swum across swollen streams. Many a traveller ended his journey in a watery grave as tiredness and heavy clothes were difficult to contend with, even for the few who were able to swim. Riders fell from their horses and drowned with what we would call alarming frequency but no doubt such hazards were accepted in those days as a fact of life. Coaches overturned or were left stranded amidst quicksands or floodwaters. Even today it is not easy to escape from an inundated vehicle and the horrors of travel then can barely be imagined. Having said that, some famous travellers covered hundreds or even thousands of miles without serious mishap. George Fox the Quaker, for example, spent a quarter of a century travelling around England with few hindrances apart from those made by his fellow creatures in endeavouring to stop him.

The increased trade generated in the Midlands caused new problems. But in Sussex travel might become impossible in the autumn and heavy loads such as timber were often left by the roadside until the spring, unless there was a hard and continuing frost which enabled transport to restart. The Duke of Somerset, whose estate at Petworth lay on one of the worst roads in the kingdom, found it necessary to keep a house at Guildford to which he could repair whenever he made the journey to London. So dreadful was the way when Prince George of Denmark travelled there from Windsor to greet King Charles of Spain that he spent fourteen hours in his coach which at frequent intervals had to be prevented from sinking into quagmires. The last nine miles took six hours.

The travellers of that time generally chose summer for their expeditions, but it was a matter of the lesser of two evils as they then had to contend with heat and dust and would often take a long break in the middle of the day. This would enable them to bait (feed) their horses as a horse cannot go all day without food. Summer storms could also pose serious problems as water in some parts of the country could rise very fast and cut off whole sections of the roads. There would then be no alternative but to swim.

To navigate his way around the country the traveller had only one road book, that produced by Ogilby in 1675, and this was too cumbersome to carry. Two hundred pages of text were interleaved with a hundred road maps and each route was set out on a series of scrolls. Roads were shown by solid lines when enclosed and by dotted lines when they crossed open country. These maps were the first to use the statute mile and showed many important features such as bridges, fords, inns and farriers.

A word about the economics of travel is probably appropriate. A coach horse would cost about £10 - £13, while a carriage horse might cost up to £20. In Oxford it was recorded that a gelding for the president of Christ's College cost £15, and "two nags, one with saddle, bridle and furniture, for Christ's College £22 4s 0d. A grey ambling gelding for the provost of King's College, Cambridge, £18." The following are some of the prices paid for trunks and luggage .. "a cloak bag 5s 6d, a trunk 8s 0d, portmantle 10s 0d and a sealskin trunk 15s 0d."

Country doctors would visit their patients on horseback and some wealthy patients in a critical condition might well detain the doctor for several days at a time. His London colleagues would consider it more dignified to keep their own Hackney carriage and horses.

Dissenting ministers would also travel round on horseback, visiting the sick, baptising infants and preaching. John Wesley, a little later, rode more miles than any other known person in England, doing just that. The Catholic priest would also travel on horseback or foot over a wide area. Being homeless, he also had to contend with all weathers. He would pass from large house to large house, cottage to cottage, sometimes openly and sometimes secretly. Often, wet, tired and hungry, he would have to lie up in a barn, coppice or wherever until nightfall, when it was safe to enter a house without fear of discovery.

Tethering post

7

Stamford to Lincoln

After my diversion to Leicester I boxed back to Stamford and then travelled north. Celia describes Stamford as a fine town built of stone and the description holds good today. The limestone is of a peculiarly pleasing dark grey colour and the place has the air of an affluent market town, now rid of the thunder of Great North Road traffic by the bypass. The town has a history of prosperity dating back to Roman times, when its importance was due to its position at the junction of two Roman roads and the fact that there was a large military settlement a mile away. Later the town became one of the five Danelaw burghs and in the fourteenth century a university was established there. A hundred years later, however, the town was destroyed by a Lancastrian army and, to make things worse, the importance of wool declined and the River Welland silted up - the old wharf buildings can still be seen. New industries were developed later which helped to restore prosperity and the position of Stamford on the Great North Road made it a key stopping place in the stage coach era. Stamford still gives the appearance of a seventeenth and eighteenth century town as, owing to the Cecils and later the Exeters, it was never allowed to develop in the way that Nottingham and Leicester did for example.

The town is a joy to visit, with numerous old buildings very much in evidence, shown off to advantage by the pedestrianisation of several areas and by the establishment of a number of town trails to guide visitors around. Narrow alleyways abound and I was delighted to find on an inn the notice ''good stabling''. A relic of the town wall is still in place at St Peter's Gate: in Celia's time of course the town gates would have been shut at night.

The open field system survived until well into the nineteenth century and any squatters who built hovels were promptly removed by the Exeters in order to preserve the power they enjoyed by returning two parliamentary candidates. Later when the railway was going north it went to Peterborough, rather than Stamford which was intended, again because of the Exeters who did not want it. So Peterborough expanded and Stamford remained static.

Celia makes reference to ''Mr Neals house'' (presumably Uffington Park) as an attractive house and park within a ring fence but it was the neighbouring Burghley House, the home of the Exeters, which she visited. She describes the house in some detail, which was first built in Tudor times and the original large kitchen and great hall survive. The state rooms in the rest of the house are in the style of the seventeenth century. Just before her visit the then Marquis of Exeter had been on several grand tours, collecting the many treasures which make the house today a veritable treasure trove.

I climbed the steps which she climbed and described as ''stone steps about twelve that all turn round; the upper Stepp is at least twenty footsteps in compass, the door you enter is of iron carvd the finest I ever saw, all sorts of leaves flowers figures birds beast wheate in the carvings''. These are fine wood carvings which were popular at about that time and can be seen in other houses on Celia's route such as Belton. The carvings at Burghley are exquisite and are the work, at least partly if not entirely, of Grinling Gibbons. She described the house accurately as it appears today ''you go thence into parlours dining roomes drawing roomes and bed-chambers, one leading out of the other at least twenty that were very large and lofty and most delicately painted on the top, each roome differing, very fine Carving in the mantlepieces and very fine paintings in pictures, but they were all without Garments or very little, that was their only fault, the immodesty of the Pictures especially in my Lords appartment; his bed-chamber was furnish'd very rich the tapistry was all blew Silke and rich gold thread''. Certainly the paintings are something of a monument to nudity. They were executed by Antonio Verrio who was employed at Burghley for twelve years and used as his models servant maids from the house. One, apparently, was loth to cooperate and he portrayed her rather cruelly and the then Dean of Windsor, with whom Verrio had fallen out, was depicted as surrounded by voluptuous maidens all in a state of undress.

Outside, the gardens have changed since Celia's time as they were then of the formal type with higher and lower walls and many fountains and statues and fine grass walks. Capability Brown changed all that, sweeping away the formal gardens and creating open landscapes, often with lakes and clumps of trees all around the house. One has to remember that, after the Civil War, labour was expensive and so many formal gardens fell into neglect. In 1753 a survey was made which stated that Burghley had a great rectangular garden south of the house and a gigantic parterre containing a complex of a bason of water, a bowling green, a grove and a wilderness, two canals, an octagonal goldfish pond, an orchard and a vineyard. The old Tudor hunting park was transformed with grids of avenues, the main ones carrying the approach to the house. The cost of the work was said to have been £30,000 and Burghley was put into the mould of the classic French or Dutch garden of the time. Celia referred to the bowling green and this is one of the few references in her journal to sports or games. The restructuring of the gardens was then still in progress. She summed up the house as ‘‘esteemed the finest house and scituation that is in England and will be very compleate when finish’d’’. Certainly the view of the house from the park, all in pale coloured stone, with its spires, roof lines, varied shapes and sheer size is unforgettable.

I rode on northwards from Stamford on a rather miserable grey, damp day. The countryside had changed from Leicestershire’s large open fields to smaller fields with stone walls, but still with sheep and cattle grazing, and I was conscious of the constant roar of traffic on the A1. The first bridleway, towards Pickworth, was bounded by stone walls and although wet under foot showed great promise. But no sooner had we started off when three deer bounded across the track, cleared the walls with ease and vanished in the direction of the A1. My fear was that Cameron would explode and buck me off in his unpredictable way. However, all was well. As we trotted on we passed two derelict farmhouses, one of them nestling against the hillside - what a perfect house it would make, I thought, not only for its position but also for its arrangement of stone barns. One could not imagine a house of such quality in the south-east being allowed to fall into disrepair.

Then after a mile or so, much to my dismay, the track petered out and this turned out to be a recurring problem over the next few days. I had always understood from hearsay that rights of way in Lincolnshire have many problems but I had not imagined the scale of blockages and obstructions that we were to encounter. Still, there was no turning back and with all ways barred I had to ride across a number of cropped fields to the nearest point of alignment, hoping that my map reading was accurate. Fortunately it turned out to be so and I ended up in the charming stone village of Pickworth. As we entered I saw the parish church perched up on a little hill opposite. The few remains of the old church stood nearby. The new church was Victorian and very plain. One felt that one could take in the whole of the interior of the church by standing and gazing about for a minute or so. It was one of the plainest parish churches that I could recall having seen.

Again and again we encountered similar problems of wire and blocked bridleways but managed to get through to the village of Clipsham by following the presumed line of the bridleway across large wheat fields. There was an additional problem caused by pheasants flying out suddenly under Cameron’s legs and startling him but after our first skirmish he settled down and took no further notice.

Shortly afterwards we passed stone quarries and I was reminded of Barnack stone from which many local churches and houses are built, as well as buildings farther afield such as the cathedrals at Norwich, Peterborough and

Bury St Edmunds, the church at Lavenham and some of the Cambridge colleges. Bury had a permanent grant of a right of way from Barnack to the wharves at the Welland ferry and stone for Norwich Cathedral was taken down the Welland, round the coast and up the Yare. The stone was also carried by carts and pack animals. The quarries were exhausted in the early sixteenth century but stone from monasteries and other disused buildings was often reused.

Clipsham is the nearest village to Stretton where Celia stayed at the house of a Mr Horsman. ''A little house ... very good plantations of trees about its stone building. Rutlandshire seems more woody and inclosed than some of the others.'' Rutlandshire is no more of course but the name lingers on in that, for instance, people will insert it in their address before the correct but prosaic Leicestershire. I was unable to locate Mr Horsman's house, but wondered if it might be the manor at Clipsham which is surrounded by woods. I later passed through the fascinating Castle Bytham with its remains of a motte and bailey, together with fishponds and signs in the fields of old ridge and furrow cultivation. History was coming alive as so often in my travels.

Just as I was about to venture onto the next bridleway I met two riders who asked where I was going. On being told, they dismissed any possibility of our getting through. They had, it appeared, made many but thus far fruitless

Woolsthorpe Manor

approaches to the county council. This setback meant that our passage to Colsterworth was restricted and diversions had to be made. This was bitterly disappointing as many rights of way were shown on the Ordnance Survey map, the scenery around was very beautiful and I was looking forward to using these routes. Time was getting on though and we had covered nothing like our projected mileage, so I decided to box Cameron to the night's stabling as we had no hope of reaching our destination by dark.

At Colsterworth I visited the manor house which is the birthplace of Sir Isaac Newton. It is owned by the National Trust and is kept lovingly by the couple who live there. They were obviously enjoying their work and were apparently always ready to show round visitors out of hours if at all practicable. Sir Isaac was a contemporary of Celia Fiennes and I wondered if she had any inkling of who he was or of how famous he was becoming. With the slow spread of news in those days it is quite conceivable that she knew nothing of him. Certainly she did not mention his name, not even the famous apple tree a cutting from which still grows in the garden.

Problems continued to abound until we joined High Dike, the local name for Ermine Street on which I would be travelling again later. Practically every bridleway on this section was wired up or ploughed out: it was the worst section of the whole ride. The amount of frustration and wasted effort caused by these obstructions of the Queen's highway, which bridleways of course are, cannot be overstated. One could easily find oneself riding twice as far as expected over certain stretches because of blockages.

Before continuing my ride I paid a visit to Grantham. It was described by Celia as "all built with stone but lies in a low bottom, the church has a very high steeple (280 feet) its seen above a great hill that is by it of a great length, and 'tis a long tyme when you see a great part of the steeple ere you come to see the church or town, it lies so in a bottom". Grantham could be described so today. It looks quite prosperous, also it is, of course, the birthplace of another famous English person, Margaret Thatcher, and the little corner shop which her father kept can still be seen. One apparently unique feature of the town is a pub with a living inn sign: it is "The Beehive" and outside, atop a post, a hive is full of a merry buzzing sound. I decided on the spur of the moment to dine at The Angel and Royal where I was given every attention and enjoyed an excellent meal. History was still very much in the air. The place is regarded as the oldest inn in England, rivalling "The Old Trip to Jerusalem" at Nottingham, and was built over 750 years ago as a hostel for the Knights Templar. I ate in the very room in which Richard III learnt of the treachery of the Duke of Buckingham in 1483 and the sense of the past being part of the present was quite palpable.

Meantimes, Cameron was also being looked after at a stables a little way up the road. The girls there loved him and he was obviously enjoying their attentions when I called for him the next day. I mentioned my problems with the bridleways to the people at the stables but it appeared that the riders in the area were happy to preserve the status quo as they were using a number of permissive routes and were satisfied with those. I regard such a policy as short-sighted as permission can be lost overnight and, more importantly, we should always be thinking of preserving our rights for future generations.

I visited Belton House which Celia mentions in passing - it had just been built when she rode by. The house is full of interest and is surrounded by beautiful parkland with views up to Ermine Street. The wood carvings, some possibly by Grinling Gibbons, hold the attention with their fine detail of leaves, flowers and wild life. One of the wood carvers, Edmund Carpenter, was paid £26 in 1688 for ‘‘a very rich chimny peece in the withdrawing roome to the Great Parlor don with varieties of fish and sheals with birds fouliage, fruit and flowers’’. Also in the house could be seen an exercise chair on which the then owner could bounce up and down as if on horseback when he was too old to enjoy that pursuit.

After visiting Belton I rode on to High Dike, joining it near Cranwell, the RAF Training College, the tower of which could be seen through the mist. There was a marked change in our riding. The problems of the last few days had fallen away and I rode for miles along a wide, well-defined way with the agger still showing in many places. I took the opportunity of riding a little faster without the need to check and recheck my map with irritating frequency. The Roman road had a width of 60-65 feet in many places and the local name of High Dike reflected the construction technique which carried the road about 6 feet above the level of the surrounding land.

Along the way I came across many place names steeped in history, such as High Dike Farm, Ermine Street Farm, and the remains of the tower of the house of the Knights Templar at Temple Bruer. This once powerful order was suppressed in 1311 and the housed passed to the Knights of St John (Hospitallers) until they were in turn swept away by the Dissolution in 1541. Bruer means heath and it is probable that a village was established here, settlers being encouraged by the Templars who needed a labour force for cultivation of their lands. I dismounted and entered the tower which was a ruin when Celia rode High Dike and had been, indeed, over a century earlier when Leland visited it. The sense of history in the place was very strong.

Another interesting local name is Byard’s Leap, of which legend says that a witch, Old Meg, lived here with her two ill-formed children or cubs in a cottage just west of the Roman road. So bad was she, the legend goes, that a former soldier in nearby Ancaster, back from the wars with his favourite horse blind Bayard, decided to rid the country of the witch. He set out for Meg's hut on old Bayard. He called to her to come out from inside and she replied ''I'll buckle my shoes an' suckle my cubs an' I'll soon be with yer, me laddie''. Soon after, she came out and the soldier cut at her with his sword. Infuriated, Old Meg sprang up behind him and her finger and toe nails went so deep into the flanks of the horse that Blind Bayard gave three enormous leaps. Retaining his seat, the old soldier turned and thrust his sword through Old Meg with such force that it pierced and killed both Old Meg and Old Bayard. Meg's cubs are said to be buried nearby.

Celia said that you can see Lincoln from six miles off, standing as it does on a very high hill. The way to it was described as being like Salisbury Plain. This has changed now, but until recently the wild and desolate Lincoln Heath had to be crossed by a traveller to Lincoln and remained uncultivated. Stories abound of travellers wandering lost on the heath. Owing to the misty conditions though I could not glimpse Lincoln until I was nearly right up to the city.

8

Lincoln to Nottingham

As I neared Lincoln the impressive way in which it stands on a high hill became evident. Defoe described the place as a decaying city and it has a little of that air today. Some of the houses around the great minster are of poor appearance and the whole aspect of the area is different from that of other cathedral cities around the country. Celia wrote of the sea that used to come up to Lincoln, called Lincoln Dike. The canal, on which the city's trade depended, fell into disuse before 1672 and this led to a decline in trade. The Roman town of Lindum Colonia was a thriving commercial centre linked to the north and south by two great canals. The Car Dyke joined the River Witham east of the city and the River Nene near Peterborough; the Fossdyke linked the Brayford Pool to the River Trent at Torksey. Growing prosperity led to the area enclosed by the city walls being increased to 96 acres.

What Defoe said, writing a few decades after Celia, was that Lincoln was "an antient, decay'd and still decaying city; it is so full of the ruins of monasteries and religious houses, that, in short, the very barns, stables, out-houses and, as they shew'd me, some of the very hog-styes, were built church-fashion". They were rough times. There is a horrifying description of one Eleanor Elsom being burnt at the stake in Lincoln, at the time of Defoe's journeys, for the murder of her husband.

I could not, unfortunately, venture inside the Minster because it had just closed. This was part of a recurring problem - by the time that I had finished a day's ride and Cameron had been settled and fed, most public buildings were closed and there was often a dead air over towns. It seemed a pity that the many tourists thronging the streets of Lincoln might never see the interior of the Minster. One thing in particular which I was sorry not to see was the carving of a gardener using an iron shod spade which evidently dates from medieval times.

I walked around the steep and narrow streets and appreciated how difficult it must have been to transfer goods by pack pony or whatever between the upper and lower parts of the city. Then I took myself to a Chinese restaurant for an early supper before returning to my place of sojourn. How readily we now take for granted the presence of Chinese restaurants in virtually every town in the country. But how difficult it would have been to have predicted such a change in our economy only two or three decades back, let alone three centuries.

I had encountered so many problems that I made a reconnaissance that evening before deciding whether to ride on to Newark. The merit of this trip was immediately evident as I lost myself leaving Lincoln. Bridleways seemed to be non-existent and then I found that the bridge over the unfordable River Witham had gone and there was no practicable alternative route. On top of this there was a whole string of other problems akin to those of the previous days. I decided to give Cameron a lift to the far side of Newark-on-Trent where I was looking forward to riding beside the Trent on quiet towpaths and bridleways. The scenery on this western side of Lincoln, near the race course, was completely different from that encountered to date, with flat fen-like land around and not a hill in sight, and waterways and dykes at every turning. Closer in to the city centre was a mass of modern roads, roundabouts, direction signs and all the usual paraphernalia of the twentieth century: I could see no merit whatsoever in attempting to ride there.

Celia comments that Newark ''is a very neate Stone built town the market place is very large and look'd fine, just by it is the Great Church which is very large and with a very high Spire, there is prayers twice a day in it; there

Jew's House, Lincoln

remaines the holes in the Church walls that the bullets made which were shott into the town in the Siege laid to it by the Parliament army in the Civil Warrs ...'' This is a particularly interesting comment as it appears to be her only reference to the Civil War. As her father, five uncles and grandfather were all involved, this is a little surprising.

The next day, just beyond Newark and with the weather somewhat improved, I unloaded Cameron with hopes high and started off by hacking through villages close to the River Trent. The route which I had selected on the map showed small lanes and, it being the Bank Holiday, I expected little traffic. It turned out, however, to my dismay, to be race day at nearby Southwell. We were passed on these narrow roads by horse box after horse box until Cameron, who is not completely traffic proof, made it clear that he had had enough. Just as a horse box came alongside us he swung round in the opposite direction and, with three big unseating bucks, nearly deposited me in the river. Fortunately, however, I managed to stay in the saddle although I was shaken by the experience, knowing perfectly well he would do the same thing again at the approach of the next large lorry.

The river was busy with pleasure craft, a feature very much of the latter part of the twentieth century. In Celia's time a few people were beginning to travel for pleasure, but leisure for the masses would be one of the enormous changes which would have to be explained to her were she to return to present day England. With a sense of thankfulness I reached the first bridleway of the day only to find a notice telling me that it was closed for the erection of a new bridge. I was bitterly disappointed but was comforted by the fact that the bridleway was being maintained. I had no alternative but to carry on along the metalled road to the next village of Hoveringham. When I got there, however, I found to my dismay that the gates to the riverside bridleway were padlocked and the gates wired on the hinge side. Even if I had managed to undo them my progress would probably have been blocked after the next field or so. There was no way that I was going to be able to ride this section to Nottingham.

Celia describes the way to Nottingham in some detail, saying that the River Trent in several places could be forded by carriages and wagons and she rode for seven or eight miles beside the river. I was so looking forward to riding these bridleways as I was sure, from her description, that they were the very ones which she had ridden with views of the ridge of hills on the other side of the river. This view has not changed much. What has changed is the freedom to ride beside the river. It is sad that the Queen's highway can apparently be blocked with impunity and one wonders what local riders are doing about it. I would certainly like to return and ride this stretch, it looked so inviting.

Celia rode near Holme Pierrepont, as I intended, and comments on the fine house and good gardens. This sixteenth century house, built of East Anglian pink brick, with its gardens and country park is still there and is open to the public. It has a special charm with its medieval rooms and family possessions. The courtyard was probably paved in Celia's time and the patterns in the parterre edged in box, all of which has recently been restored. Other restoration work has been carried out and plants with grey leaves have been planted to help create a fascinating display of colour throughout the year.

Nottingham was Celia's favourite town, which she used as a basis for comparison "... the neatest town I have seen, built of stone and delicate large and long Streetes much like London and the houses lofty and well built, the market place is very broad - out of which runns two very large streetes much like Holborn but the buildings finer and there is a Pyaza all along one side of the Streetes, with stone pillars for walking that runns the length of the Streete which is a mile long". In a recent party political broadcast on television, the then Prime Minister, Margaret Thatcher, held up Nottingham as an excellent example of local government working properly. The similarity with Celia's description was so striking that one wonders whether Mrs Thatcher had been aware of it when she prepared her broadcast. Certainly Nottingham does have a good appearance and one can see how the title ''Queen of the Midlands'' arose. It has long been a centre for the manufacture of bricks and tiles and also for the weaving of stockings and spun glass: Celia saw a coloured swan and buttons being made. The now important industry of tobacco production had not begun in Celia's time, of course.

She, unusually, stayed on this occasion at the Blackmoor's Head and not in someone's home. She comments in some detail about Sir Thomas Willoughbys' fine house Wollaton Hall. The house still exists and has been little altered externally since Celia's time; the Elizabethan gardens, however, have gone which is a pity because they were unique for their period. The house, outbuildings, courtyard and gardens were designed as an entity; four beds surrounded a central fountain at the time of her visit and the second garden was laid out as a knot garden. Wollaton was known as an example of a type of design which had become standard practice in France by the second half of the sixteenth century.

It is perhaps surprising that she does not comment on the fact that the house was in the middle of a coalfield which was developed on the estate. The Willoughbys were an enterprising family as glass was blown on the estate also and woad was cultivated as the basis for a local dyeing industry. In addition they had an interest in the mining and forging of iron in South Derbyshire.

There is a fine painting of the hall by Jan Siberechts executed in 1697, showing the house set among open, hilly countryside with the formal gardens which obviously delighted Celia. This Dutchman painted other gardens which Celia visited on her travels: it was a period when many gardens were being recorded in this way. Sir Thomas was a friend of the botanist John Ray who was a great collector of ‘‘phisicall plants’’, that is plants for curing ailments which would often be grown in physic gardens, of which there is an example in Chelsea which still flourishes today. Indeed, the advice of Richard Pratt who set up the Chelsea garden was sought in establishing the physic garden at Wollaton. This was a time of great gardening activity and seeds were being sent to this country from all over the world.

I had had such problems riding over the past five days that I did wonder whether it was even practicable to continue our journey. The thought of going northwards and encountering even worse problems daily was very depressing and so I decided, rather than continue northwards, to box Cameron to Scarborough and then ride southwards back towards Nottingham. So even if I still found the bridleways to be blocked, at least I was heading towards home.

9

Scarborough to York

When planning this section of the ride, I decided to leave out Hull and Burton Agnes (a house which was owned by one of Celia's relations) for the simple reason that there were virtually no linking bridleways in the area and a slog along roads would have been involved. So I boxed Cameron for the long hop northwards from Nottingham and stayed with a friend on the North Yorkshire Moors before resuming the ride from Scarborough.

Before setting off on the ride, I climbed as Celia did to the ruined castle perched above the town. The walls encompass sixteen acres which, in her time, fed many beasts including milch cows. Today the castle is a tourist attraction as, indeed, is the town itself. Scarborough still boasts good firm sands on which, as Celia points out, one can walk for five or six miles. I gazed down on the half-moon harbour mole but could see only a few vessels rather than the many colliers and men of war of Celia's time. The country was then still at war with France and the warships were in convoy.

Raising my eyes I could see the church ''in the most eminent place above all the town'' and groups of people were chatting in the calm evening sunshine. Near them boys were playing in a portion of the churchyard which had been grassed over. Bringing my gaze down to my very feet, I stared at the well kept grave of Anne Bronte, who lies buried just within the churchyard wall. How strange it is to be aware of the unfolding pattern of history which was, as it were, to dot ''i''s and cross ''t''s of things which Celia saw. In her time, people were visiting the town to take the waters although the spa buildings were not erected until three years later. The springs bubble up all over the sands, she reported. The town was also famous, according to Celia and to Defoe, for its codling. At the end of the day, when at last I sat down for dinner, codling was on the menu so I naturally chose it. It was excellent, although I did not ascertain where it had come from.

Celia probably rode south of the hills which lie inland from Scarborough. I rode in a northerly direction over the hills and through the forest of which she would have known nothing as it was planted only this century: in her time, the hills would have been barren moorland. It was a hot day and I rode slowly in shirtsleeves on the very stony tracks. Climbing and descending the hills and criss-crossing many streams, I was pleased to note that Cameron was going boldly into water and was obviously enjoying the experience. At times I rode along the very streams with water splashing up to his girth. He was taking many opportunities to drink while he was in the water and this also I was pleased about, as frequent drinking for horses on long rides is essential as it saves them from the ever present danger of dehydration.

Sheep abounded everywhere and often jumped down from higher ground onto the track in front of us and then into the valley below. Cameron was still a little jumpy about sheep but was beginning to take them in his stride. We followed many narrow tracks which hugged the hillside and at times I was apprehensive lest Cameron should stumble and we fall into the valley: he lacked the experience of the Spanish horses which I had ridden in the Sierra Nevadas in Spain. Through Trouts Dale I had the most beautiful views and at Basin Howe I came across some early earthworks which were deep and extensive, stretching southwards. By then the view had expanded into all directions and was quite unforgettable. We dropped down into a valley, only to climb again and then pass through gateways where cattle were quietly cropping the grass - mercifully the gates could be opened readily from Cameron's back.

We had reached a point of no return when I realised that a bull was running out with Friesian cows. After an earlier experience in Suffolk, I was full of apprehension. However, the bull did not even bother to lift his head and it was with a sigh of relief that I closed the next gate behind us. As we left the forest, I lost my way briefly and had to cross and recross a stream by High Dalby. I was pleased to see chalkland flowers including many orchids and foxgloves in the forest as I rode. We later crossed the line of the North Yorkshire Moors Railway, the longest private railway in the country, and shortly afterwards heard the penetrating blast of the whistle of a steam locomotive. I was thankful that we were well out of the way. We climbed steeply again to Newton on Rawcliffe where I was staying the night with an old friend, a Yorkshire expatriate, who had bought a small manor house and farm, renovated it and was in process of converting some of the buildings into holiday accommodation for horses and riders. She is an authority on rights of way and I had the pleasure of her company for the following day on my ride. That evening, once the horses had been fed and settled and we had studied our route for the next day, we were able to talk about the old roads of Yorkshire and I took the opportunity of

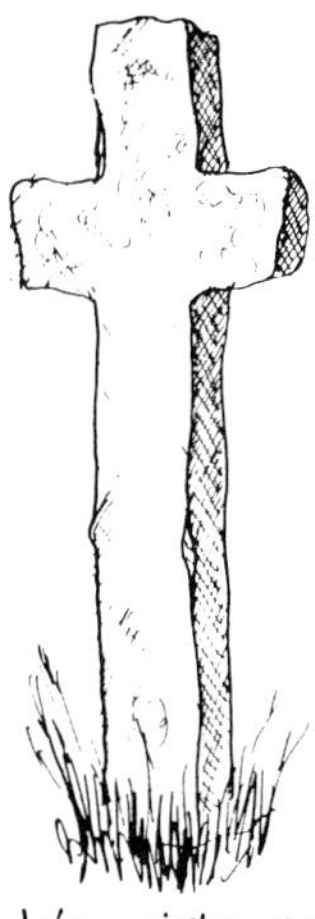
Wayside cross

marking up my maps accordingly.

Close to Newton passes Wade's Causeway which is part of a Roman road, probably from York to the vicinity of Whitby, which is thought to date back to AD 80. One use for this road in past times was for the transportation of Whitby jet which was, and still is, made up into ornaments. The road was completely overgrown and buried until it was uncovered by an eighteenth century historian. In parts remains of it can still be seen, sixteen feet wide and with large foundation stones.

I was delighted how well Cameron coped with the terrain as he had not had to cope with steep slopes before and he seemed happy enough to go up and down the hills all day with no after effects or even tiredness. However, at the bottom of the first hill, he did stop and put his head round as if to say "you don't expect me to carry you up there do you?". Just north of Rawcliffe I was fascinated to see a well preserved wayside cross. These crosses were probably partly religious in origin and partly a means of guiding people across the moors.

Mounting block

In the days of horse and cattle transport the steepness of the terrain made it necessary to devise special ways of transporting loads. In many areas only pack animals would have been used, but in 1662 the legal draught for a wheeled vehicle was increased to seven horses or eight oxen with loads limited to 30 hundredweight in summer. Then in 1696 the law allowed an extra horse to be added. In the mid-1840s, in the Vale of Pickering, the Rev J C Atkinson wrote of his astonishment at seeing a team of ten horses and ten oxen. He noted that the oxen could work for longer hours than horses but that the stony going played havoc with their cloven feet. It is possible that Celia saw such large teams at work although she makes no reference to them.

Apart from the large estates, this part of Yorkshire appeared to consist of small farms with cattle and sheep and it was not until we got farther south near York that I saw arable land with vegetables being grown.

On my way to visit Malton without Cameron I came upon a mounting block at the edge of the pavement. How I wish that these useful objects could be sited in both town and country, as getting onto a horse from the ground is not always easy and many gates simply cannot be opened and closed from horseback. Celia described Malton as "a pretty large town, built of stone but poor''. The town had clearly gone up in the world as it had an air of prosperity with the market place still there and very busy. One could imagine the market place as it would have been in Celia's time with stalls surrounding the church, as this was common practice all over the country.

I did not visit the Yorkshire towns in the order in which she did and indeed some I had to miss out altogether as I explained earlier. My travelling companion and I rode on from Malton through the Castle Howard estate. This house was not built in Celia's time, although the plans were in process of being drawn up. Castle Howard is a re-creation of an Italian style house on the North Yorkshire Moors and the countryside was modified by Vanbrugh from its original ''bushes, bogs and briars'' to avenues of limes, open grassland and clumps of trees.

The park has vast gatehouses which are certainly in keeping with a castle, together with a temple of four winds, an obelisk, sham fortifications and a pyramid. The layout of the park is most unusual in that the main avenue is to the west of the house and does not lead directly to it, although a more imposing avenue with its obelisks and gatehouses it would be hard to imagine. Our approach to the park took us through the woods to the north and provided some delightful riding. Cameron was suddenly ''set alight'' by the excitement of the soft peaty going and began weaving his way in and out of the trees, the sort of going which he always thoroughly enjoys. We emerged from the woods and the view presented to us was as Vanbrugh obviously intended: we simply had to pause for a few moments to enjoy it.

The way ahead was not clearly defined but it took us only a few minutes to sort out our route because, fortunately, we were using the larger scale map. We descended a steep hill, only to climb again. The going became hard and stony and less pleasant for the horses and also the gates were all difficult once again. We took it in turns to dismount to open some; others could be managed without dismounting but it was a question of heaving and pulling half broken gates and posts. Time and time again we nearly fell from the saddle in an endeavour to shut and re-tie gates. The problem was accentuated by the fact that we were both feeling the effect of old injuries incurred from riding and walking accidents.

As we neared a farmhouse on the estate a farmer shouted out for us to stop. He thought that he had recognised my large chesnut horse as belonging to someone who persistently strayed from the bridleway and galloped across his fields, cutting corners and scattering sheep. He at once realised that he was mistaken and we assured him that we would keep to the bridleway. However, when I found how stony and unpleasant the track was I did have some sympathy with the rider who strays onto the grass.

Our approach to the hall afforded us with views of the temple and mausoleum and then the pyramid which were nothing short of theatrical. From the gatehouse at the top of the avenue a completely new vista had opened up; the rise and fall of the road with its gatehouses and obelisks filled our vision and we paused again to admire the vista. We then had a final canter together down the avenue, at the end of which our ways parted and I said good-bye to Elizabeth. Unusually, Cameron began to whinny and fuss at the loss of his companion, the two horses had got on well together, and at the same time his discomfort was made worse by horse flies descending on him and biting viciously. His thin skin quickly comes up into great bumps and weals which can stay up for a couple of days and so he was jumpy and uncomfortable for the rest of the day's ride.

So far all the bridleways which I had encountered in Yorkshire had been signposted, often with waymarks as well, and unobstructed. Across tracts of open land, however, careful and accurate map-reading was necessary. This is not so easy as it may sound, as reading a map on the back of a horse is a quite different matter from reading one seated at a table. Cameron has been taught to stand still when I open a map on his back since he was a four year old , but even so, he tends to fidget and try to grab pieces of hedgerow to eat. Cobs, I should explain in passing, are browsers by nature, quite unlike thoroughbreds who are much more choosy over their food.

Newby Hall

The scenery changed dramatically as we left the hills behind us and descended to the Great Yorkshire Plain with its orderly fields, cattle, sheep and arable crops. The hills had quickly disappeared from view and we travelled on to the small market town of Easingwold where we were staying the night. At the end of a long, hot but enjoyable day one looks forward eagerly to creature comforts like a bath and a meal once Cameron has been settled and fed.

We arrived at the stables where we had booked and found two separate yards with horses in the stables and fields but not a soul about. The only sign of life apart from the horses was two noisy guard dogs. One can imagine my frustration and annoyance at finding no one to meet us. However, in desperation I found an empty box and put Cameron in there. Fortunately, I always carry feed in the truck and so was able to settle him for the night on the assumption that he was in the right stable. To make things worse he had lost a shoe during all this activity. He is prone to this: when he gets excited he somehow manages to stamp hard with one forefoot on the other and pull off what is ostensibly a tight and firmly fitting shoe. I then set to and located the stable owner in the next village. The booking had been made through a third party and it turned out that some confusion had arisen as a result. All was well with the stable I was using, mercifully, and the owner recommended a farrier to put back the shoe. It was important that the horse be sorted out completely before I could settle down for the evening and so I next went to find the farrier.

Unfortunately, he had just returned from holiday and could not, or would not, help and I was still not out of the wood. So it was back to the stable owner and another farrier was located. He agreed to do the job the next morning early although it was Sunday and so I was able, with great relief, to go to the hotel.

When eventually I reached The George Inn where I had booked I found the whole town alive with people and brass bands and I had to fight my way in to reception. The fact that I was carrying my saddle and bridle together with my luggage didn't help matters and it was the subject of some good humoured banter from some men propping up the bar. I had arrived in the middle of a brass band competition. The bands were marching round the town in turn, playing their set pieces and excitement was running high. As I prepared for dinner, the competition had finished but many of the musicians were playing hymn tunes beneath our window. The effect was quite magical. Brass bands are part of a strong tradition of nonconformity in the north and I felt sure that Celia would have approved had she been with me.

I went down to dinner through a milling throng of musicians, local people and tourists drinking and talking in the bar and around the tables outside. The noise and bustle was enormous but the world of hooliganism and vandalism was a million miles away.

The next morning, as I prepared to continue, I was pleased to note that there was hardly any litter to be seen and one man was able to clear up what there was in a few minutes. I was expected at Newby Hall at about midday and so, allowing for two and a half or three hours' riding, there was a great deal to do. Having gone to the stables to feed Cameron, I returned to the hotel to enjoy an excellent but hurried Yorkshire breakfast, pack and check out. Then it was back to the stables again to load Cameron and visit the farrier some miles farther on. Although it was early Sunday morning he had already left to do another job and I had to wait for his return. He was back within a few minutes and his professional appearance and friendly manner immediately put me at my ease. As he replaced the shoe he plied me with questions about my ride and chatted about how to cope with hoof problems. It is axiomatic that good feet are essential for a long-distance horse and so comments and advice are always worth listening to. When he had finished I asked him how much I owed and was surprised to be told "nothing". The whole episode was an excellent example of what the textbooks call the Protestant work ethic.

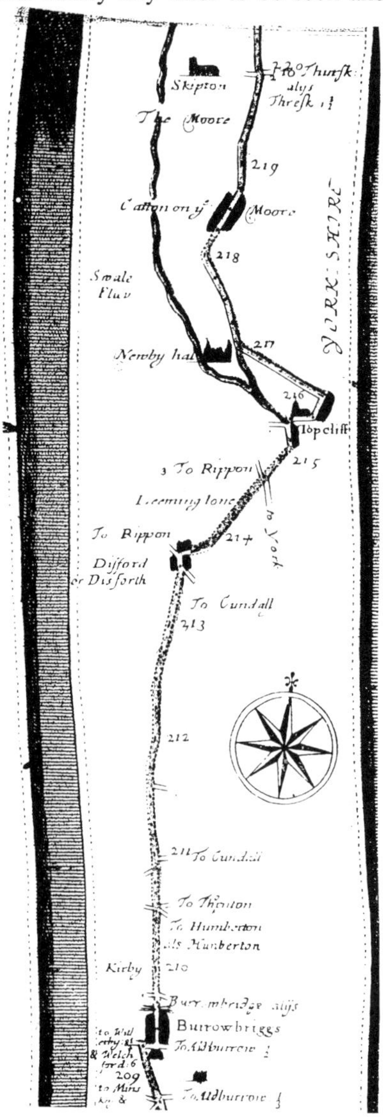

A John Ogilby map

At last we were on our way again. The weather had changed completely, the warmth of the previous night had gone and it was chilly as we journeyed on to the small town of Boroughbridge. This town traces its origins back to Roman times when it was important for several reasons. It stood at the junction of the

Roman roads to the north and to York and retained its importance after the Romans left as, for at least three centuries, it was a port through which lead from the Pennines, along with other goods, was transported to York or Selby for transhipment to London and abroad. Indeed a network of packhorse tracks and waggon roads became established for carrying commodities such as food, wool, wine, dyes and medications. The bridge over the River Ure is mentioned as early as 1145, but whether this was the same bridge which Celia saw I do not know. Certainly Celia comments on the large stone bridge which is still there. How well constructed these old bridges must have been to stand up to the twentieth century traffic as they do. One has to remember that in the seventeenth century virtually all the bridges in the south were made of wood with the exception of London Bridge.

Our next stopping place was Newby Hall, home of Mr & Mrs Robin Compton. I had looked forward to this visit for many months because of Celia's detailed descripton of the hall and gardens and it was a thrill to ride through the park just as she would have done. Sheep abounded and I was pleased to note that Cameron had settled down and was not unduly perturbed by their presence. I managed to trot steadily on, not only to make up time but also to keep warm as it was still chilly in contrast to the previous day. The man on duty at the gate had been briefed and rang for the administrator to come and meet us. We were made very welcome and in no time were established in the corner of the car park and Cameron became the centre of attraction for visitors for the next couple of hours which, of course, he loved.

As he was relaxed and content to stand quietly I was able to spend a little time visiting the hall and gardens. I quickly understood why Celia wrote at great length about the place. The gardens cover some twenty five acres and must be one of the finest privately owned gardens in the country. I took great pleasure in walking through the rose gardens, including one in red and white entitled The Wars of the Roses, the statue walk, the herbaceous borders, the rock garden and so on which drop down to the tranquil River Ure.

In Celia's time, the gardens were formally laid out under the Dutch influence. Many trees were being imported for gardens and Peter Aram, the head gardener, went to The Netherlands in 1695-6 and returned with lime trees, two thousand elms, a similar number of beeches and twenty seven fruit trees, together with seeds. Trees were being grown in the south of England but importation was still common in the north. From Celia's detailed description, there were flower gardens, and gardens with statues and squares full of borders of flowers, with gravel walks between grass plots. When she visited, the house had just been constructed at the direction of the owner Sir Edward Blackett, who was MP for Ripon. There is in the house a record of the wages, including

Cook £10 a year, Gardener £16, Coachman £5, Miss Blackett's woman £2.10.00 and Kitchen Maid £2.

After Celia's visit, the next twenty five years saw great changes. The house passed to William Weddell and he made the grand tour, which was then highly popular, in 1765-6. After his return he made contact with most of the leading neo-classical architects with a view to enlarging the house. He added two wings and inspired much of the interior of the house as we see it today. Certainly the interior is quite dramatic, with high colourful rooms, many beautiful pieces of furniture and superb detailed finish everywhere.

Leaving Newby, I made my way to Hewick Bridge, another fine stone arched bridge which Celia rode over. It was in her time in process of being repaired because of the damage caused by the force of water following heavy rain. The work was apparently carried out by building wooden structures upstream to break the force of the current. It seems that drainage must have improved or perhaps the reconstruction work was very thorough: in any event it is difficult to conceive of the present structure suffering any damage from the river current.

I continued my ride southwards and made my way to Copgrove along quiet lanes and bridleways. One of these was marked by a "Private Road" sign and I hesitated, wondering whether I had read my map correctly and it really was a bridleway. There was no mistake and on riding down it I discovered that it passes through a racing stable. It seemed evident that the owners were intent on keeping other riders and walkers off this right of way: the owners were no doubt motivated by considerations of security and virus precautions but this is not an acceptable reason for trying to keep people away.

The reason for my visit to Copgrove was that Celia had visited St Mungo's Well there which went out of use two hundred years ago. She bathed in the water and describes in detail how she wore her Bath garments which, we learn from her entry on her visit to that city, were made of fine yellow canvas which was stiff and had large sleeves like a parson's gown. The idea was that the water filled the garment so that it ballooned out and did not cling to the body. There was in those days a concern that the body should not be seen or discerned, a notion which of course persisted until quite recent times. When she emerged from the well she put on a flannel garment and went to bed, presumably at the Hall as the place is even today only a tiny hamlet. She claimed to derive benefit from the treatment, especially in easing a pain in her head from which she suffered.

In her journal she recounts the story of how the well came to be built. A baby, which was found by the churchwardens in this place, grew to manhood and fame. He had always used the spring to wash himself and he then built a wall to create a well in which he is said to have effected cures of many diseased people. After the man's death more and more people continued to visit the well, so much so that because of the resulting inconvenience the owners stopped up the well and forbade people to visit the site. However, the story goes on, the owners had many judgments visited upon them and eventually the spring broke through the ground and they had to reopen the well. The well then was about four or five yards square at the brim with a walkway of broad stone around it. There were four or five steps down to the bottom; if one knelt on a stone in the bottom the water would come as far as one's chin. It was apparently exceedingly cold, so much so that one could not bear to stay in for more than two or three minutes.

I liked the small church which dates in part back to the time of the Knights Hospitallers. In the churchyard I noticed the grave of a man who served as churchwarden for seventy three years, a remarkable achievement which seemed in tune with the coming together of past and present which had become the theme of my journey.

Yorkshire cruck barn

As I rode on I noticed that the scenery had become less dramatic. In the main though the farming pattern had not changed and many sheep and cattle were still to be seen. There were still many gates to open and close and many fords to cross. The tracks were less stony and I took the opportunity of trotting and cantering along some stretches. Celia would have looked on a different landscape as this area was not enclosed until after 1730, several decades after she passed through. It would have been a less neat landscape than I saw, with open moorland, scattered farm buildings and no hedges. It was only after enclosure took place that neat farmsteads, hedges and small fields appeared.

Cameron was stabled that night in a small stone built stable on a farm near Ripon which was a long way from the road and approached by a steep and stony track. However, he was comfortable enough even though he had to bend his head low to enter. Once he was settled, which did not take long, I set off to visit Ripon, where the busy Thursday market is still declared open by the Wakeman ringing a handbell at llam and where he also sounds curfew at 9pm daily, a custom which is at least a thousand years old. Indeed, Ripon is the second oldest city in the country, with a charter of incorporation dated 886 granted by Alfred the Great. The city is still a remarkably small place with a population of only 12,000. It gained some importance in the fourteenth and fifteenth centuries for its woollen manufacture, but later the principal business activity became fairs for horses, horned cattle and sheep, and tanning and leather working also prospered as a result. Old street names in Ripon can still be seen as a reminder of those times, such as Kirkgate, Fishergate, Horsefair and so on. The market area has been partially infilled but otherwise it is largely as Celia would have seen it and it is still some two acres in extent. She comments that there were plenty of inns and later that evening I ate at one, The Unicorn, where as I was in Yorkshire I opted for the traditional starter of Yorkshire pudding with onion gravy, and very good it was.

Celia comments also on the market day when provisions were plentiful and cheap. Shoulders of veal were not fatty and smaller than the meat in London, and a good quarter of lamb could be bought for 9d or 10d. ''Crawfish 2d a Dozen, so we bought them.''

Celia visited the Minster, which is still situated on the very edge of the city, and remarks on the hangings and the large painting over the altar. Sadly, yet again, the Minster was shut and I had to content myself with walking round the outside and studying the superb west front. In her time churches and cathedrals were probably never locked and so this would not have been a problem for her.

All this sounds very attractive and so it was, but unfortunately I could not obtain accommodation in the city and had to settle for a a sad motel which was once a coaching inn and gave the feeling of past glories. It was adequate and the sheets on the bed were clean but I couldn't help wondering whether it was not an occasion on which I should have produced my own silk sheets just as Celia would have done. However, there were no frogs, slow-worms or snails such as she found in her room at Ely.

Before I fell asleep I thought about the decline of the coaching inn which was caused by the rapid development of the railways during the nineteenth century. There is a remarkable series of books by a John James Hissey about driving around the country during that period and, time after time, he recounts sad stories of visiting hotels which used to be thriving coaching establishments but which had shrunk almost to nothing, hanging on to a pathetic existence by a mere thread. At one, for instance, the one in-house servant whom the place could support was seen to scuttle out to buy the necessary provisions once he and his companions had placed their order for a meal. The ostler at the place was such an incompetent zombie, he had of course hardly any horses to tend to, that he cleaned the brass fittings of their horses' harness with boot blacking and, to make things worse, the calamity was not spotted until later the following day.

However, I was tired enough to sleep well and forget my surroundings as it had been a long and trying day. Before continuing with my ride the next morning, I decided to visit nearby Harrogate and Knaresborough. I had not appreciated that the former was once a village on the outskirts of the latter and grew to its present size and prosperity on the back of the springs which were found to abound there. The situation is similar to that of Tunbridge Wells and Tonbridge in Kent, both of which Celia visited on a separate ride later.

She approached Harrogate across the common from Knaresborough which she describes as being all marshy and wet and having as a result to make a compass of two miles. She went there to take the waters but she could not force her horse near the Old Sulphur Well because of the offensive odour which she likened to carrion or a jakes, or loo as we would say today. There were three other springs then, the Chalybeate (iron) Spring, a Spring of Common Water and a fourth which had a petrifying quality. She dwelt at great length on the value of this and other spas, which is not surprising when one recalls that her travels were made partly for the benefit of her health. The seaside had yet to be discovered and the spas provided a means by which the well off could seek to improve their health. Indeed it has been suggested, probably correctly, that this belief in the benefit of spring waters was a continuation of water worship which had prehistoric origins.

Celia became quite an authority on the subject and wrote at length on the relative merits of each type of water. Really though there can have been little wrong with her in view of the distances which she rode and the fact that she could tackle virtually any type of food which was offered. Harrogate increased in importance after Celia's time but today the spa is no more, although the Royal Baths serve as a reminder of a bygone age, even though they are no more than a building which provides meeting rooms, refreshment facilities and so on. The whole place does have a wonderfully old fashioned air.

Celia refers to the common which is situated between Knaresborough and Harrogate. This tract of land was enclosed by Act of Parliament in 1770 but two hundred acres were set aside for the benefit of people visiting the wells and to give free public access to all. This parcel of land, known as The Stray, is one of the many attractive features of Harrogate and has an altogether distinctive air. The Stray is, however, now mown and neat and has lost the feel of common land.

Knaresborough has been described as a poor relation of Harrogate. This is unkind as it is an attractive little workaday town which boasts of a dramatic gorge near its centre through which the River Nidd flows. I was thrilled to cross the same bridge over the river which she had crossed and to note the black appearance of the water as she had, the black appearance being caused by the presence nearby of iron and sulphur mines. Close to the bridge is the petrifying well which, because of the limestone content, turns absorbent objects apparently to stone. Celia also comments on the houses built into the rock; they are still to be seen and very attractive they look, giving the area by the riverside something of a Spanish atmosphere. It was with pleasant memories of the two very different but attractive places of Harrogate and Knaresborough that I left the area to continue my journey to the next staging post of the cathedral city of York.

Farmhouse, North Yorkshire

10

York to Castleford

I left Cameron at the stables for my visit to York, the thought of riding him round the one-way systems with traffic speeding past and milling throngs of tourists everywhere filled me with horror. I was delighted to find that the Minster did not close until 8.30pm and so I was able to gaze at the same great east window, depicting the beginning and end of the world using scenes from Genesis and Revelation, which had so excited Celia. The sense of wonderment was enhanced by recalling that the window was already nearly three hundred years old when she saw it and that people have worshipped in the building for about a millenium. The sense of wonderment was even further enhanced by the fact that the Minster contains half the medieval stained glass in the country and that the whole building came within an ace of total destruction in the fire of 1984. In Celia's time the broad aisles were used by fashionable people to walk after evensong as there was no convenient park or garden near and this led her to complain about the state of cleanliness inside the building. Outside the Minster, she comments unfavourably on the narrowness of the streets and how they lent a mean appearance to the place. Times have changed and most visitors today would find that narrowness to lend enchantment to the scene. Her comment on the way in which the place is divided by rivers is still relevant today. I found myself staying on one side of the River Ouse and my horse on the other. To get from one place to the other involved a long detour and a glance at the map shows that there are few river crossings around the city even today.

York has, of course, become a major tourist attraction and I suppose one must see Celia as one of the early tourists, looking at and commenting on things which in totality had been seen by very few people indeed. Touring round England was gaining in popularity and a few people were begining to visit from overseas. While I was visiting York I stayed at a guest house which from the brochure sounded rather special and I was looking forward to it after the previous night's rather grotty accommodation. As I approached my heart sank at the sight of a gloomy building and an overgrown garden. Clearly the place had fallen on hard times but the odd thing was that it seemed as though the guests had not changed, they were still very much the oldish rather U people that one immediately recognises as English types anywhere in the world. However we were made very welcome and had no complaints and indeed a plus point was that there was a lift for disabled guests, something that is the exception even in these enlightened times. Going to my room, I found that the eccentric atmosphere extended there; there were no sheets on the bed and the loo was in a cupboard which one had to bend low to enter. The whole place, I came to realise, had the feel of an Agatha Christie crime story. In my tired state I almost expected to learn of the sudden death of one of the guests and when the door of the huge wardrobe in my room opened creakily of its own volition I nearly jumped. By the way, the detective story as such was, of course, unknown to Celia and a century and a half would have to elapse before Wilkie Collins was to write his masterpiece ''The Moonstone'' and inspire thousands of other writers to explore this new genre.

Nothing untoward happened, however, and after a good night's sleep I went off to the stables the other side of the river to check Cameron. He had been well cared for and I spent some time chatting to the young proprietor who was working very hard to build up a high class equestrian establishment for which there was an evident demand in the area. I came away clutching details of a forthcoming ride across China which was to be led by a man who is widely known as a slightly crazy Frenchman. Before saddling Cameron to resume my ride southwards I took the opportunity of visiting the nearby ''Bishops Seate'' beside the Ouse as Celia had: little had apparently changed and it is still the Bishop's palace today.

After this brief excursion I returned to the stables to fetch Cameron and I boxed him across the Ouse, unloaded him and headed south across Marston Moor, riding by bridleways to Bilton, Healaugh and Tadcaster. What an easy day! All the tracks were open and the going was straightforward except that at one point naughty Cameron got up to one of his tricks: there was a stone trough at the side of a bridleway which he shied at violently as we cantered past, very nearly depositing me in a field of wheat. The scenery had changed yet again, with wheat, barley and vegetables being grown in more profusion. We were able to ride right to the outskirts of Tadcaster by bridleways without having to go through any suburban sprawl.

As I entered Tadcaster there was a further change: new houses were being built close to the bridleway and I found myself back with dramatic suddenness in the modern world of busy roads, shops, petrol stations and the famous brewery. We needed a short break but the surroundings were most unsuitable. However, a good Samaritan appeared in the form of a man who emerged from a house by the bridleway and asked if he could be of assistance. It transpired that he was a horse lover who had lived in the house for years, before the nearby houses were built, and was only too pleased to let Cameron graze in his yard.

In Celia's time Tadcaster was a good town for travellers, with many inns and suppliers of provisions, standing on a large river, The Wharfe, which could not be crossed in wet weather except by boat and even in summer there were problems as the going was very deep. Defoe made a similar comment thirty years later. In the time of Celia and Defoe, this part of Yorkshire was one of the centres of the woollen industry. He said in his journal that " ...we could see that at almost every house there was a tenter, and almost on every tenter a piece of cloth, or a kersie or shalloon, for which there are three articles of that country's labour ... as every clothier must keep a horse, perhaps too to fetch and carry for the use of his manufacture, to fetch home his wool and his provisions from the market, to carry his yarn to the spinners, his manufacture to the fulling mill..." It is worth recalling that we still use the word "tenter" in the phrase "on tenterhooks": they were originally of course the hooks on the tenter by means of which the cloth was attached.

Within this area and southwards lies a ridge of magnesium limestone which led to the establishment of other industries. There were chalk quarries with kilns for burning lime and for making raw material for whitening; there were also sand and gravel pits and brick manufacture was carried on as well. Small lime kilns were found in profusion in all chalk areas up until relatively recent times when the process came to be carried out on an industrial scale. The main outlet for the limestone was as fertiliser; chalk or calcium carbonate was burned under controlled conditions in order to remove carbon dioxide gas and leave lime or calcium oxide as the residue.

The weather had changed for the better as I rode on southwards on the Old London Road, which is now a bridleway, but to my consternation there were lorries rumbling around all over the place. My heart sank as I feared that I would have to confront these monsters on the narrow track ahead. However, they were serving limestone quarries close by but luckily just off my route and did not constitute a problem.

My greatest difficulty turned out to be at a remote farm a few miles farther on. What an odd feel the place had, people stared at me from a distance with evident suspicion and I wanted to hurry through but could not because of the large numbers of sheep, goats, geese and many breeds of chickens and bantams running around loose. To cap it all there was a pony stallion in a field with his mares which he left and galloped up to a flimsy fence which was all that kept him away from us. He stood there snorting and then started to gallop up and down. By this time Cameron was thoroughly worked up and very jumpy and I had to use all my strength to get him past, resorting to my whip. While this was going on I became aware of the fact that I was being watched by men standing on stacks and surveying me with cold stares. The feeling was altogether horrible, rather as though they had some guilty secret and resented my intrusion. To my great relief I did eventually manage to get past and continued to ride without further hazard for the rest of the day to the nearest convenient point to Castleford, Ferrybridge and Pontefract.

Ford at Much Hadham

Setting off on Ermine Street

Bridge at Duddington

Near Graveley, Cambs

Near Pickworth, Lincs

View from Ball Cross, Derbys

Plague grave, Eyam

Monsal Dale, Derbys

Ebbing and Flowing Well, Derbys

Cameron beside the North Sea

Cameron

Rowan ambling through North Suffolk

11

Castleford to Chesterfield

Pontefract appears in Domesday; it was an important trading place and stood close to where the north-south Roman road crossed the river at a ford. There was a market area which is now built over but which can still be detected through such names as Woolmarket, Beast Fair and Cornmarket. The town is today effectively part of one entity together with Castleford and Knottingley, they being divided only by the M62 and the A1.

Celia notes the roads hereabouts as having heavy bottoms and long miles and her observation is that people could not direct one to the next place. I had the benefit of the Ordnance Survey maps of course whereas all Celia would have had would have been the Ogilby maps which were more suited to the dining room table than for use on the back of a horse. But I was not able to test the knowledge of the local folk as I met no one of whom to ask directions had I needed to do so. We know that Celia was sometimes confused when she sought directions by the use of local words unfamiliar to her. For instance, ''gate'' was used to mean a way, in line with the Danish word ''gata'', and ''geat'', which became ''yate'' in common speech, to mean a movable barrier. Whether these words are still in use I was not able to judge.

Our way took us on to Doncaster via Wentbridge and we were able to locate the house which had belonged to Sir John Wentworth from Elmsall and Brodsworth. The hall is close to a bridleway which had been partially ploughed out but was passable. Crossing the motorway, the bridleway passes a colliery and goes along a Roman ridge into Doncaster. Doncaster, even in Celia's time, was a large town and she describes the streets as good, with a handsome market cross and a good large meeting place. A vast amount of building took place in the nineteenth century and Doncaster changed a great deal, but the original town can still be traced through the old street names. What a godsend they can be to the student of history.

The next section, from Doncaster to Blyth, is completely devoid of bridleways running south and it appeared from the Ordnance Survey map that there were not even any quiet lanes along which I could ride, so I boxed Cameron up to Blyth. Celia describes the ways going south as heavy and sandy but after the hard, stony limestone tracks of North Yorkshire I found the going to be much easier. It enabled us to proceed at a smart trot, partly through woods and partly through farm land. I had noted on the map that one of the bridleways disappeared where it crossed a disused airfield and on reaching that point I found to my surprise a notice to the effect that one had to be sure the runway was clear before crossing, as testing was in progress. Whether they were testing cars or planes was not made clear but several cars did speed past at exceptionally high speed. Waiting for a gap between cars I took a deep breath and urged Cameron across as quickly as possible. What a contrast there was between the quiet countryside around us and these speeding vehicles. I wondered again what Celia's reaction would have been had she been able to return and stand there beside me.

Shortly afterwards our way took us through Osberton Hall Estate which is well known to equestrians because of the three day events which are held there. I paused to look at the imposing jumps but decided that they were not for us and we continued on our way. The scenery had softened somewhat with undulating countryside and good tracks and the bridleway took us right to the very outskirts of Worksop where there was a dramatic transition from country to town, from agriculture to mining and industry. This was a continuing pattern throughout this area of the Midlands.

We continued by riding through the northern end of Sherwood Forest where again the going changed, this time to peaty wooded tracks which Cameron so loves. This was the fastest riding since we had left Leicestershire and it was thoroughly enjoyable in the warm sunshine. To anyone in this day and age Sherwood Forest is of course syonymous with Robin Hood and we did partially follow the modern recreational route of Robin Hood's Way. It may seem curious to us that Celia Fiennes makes no reference to Sherwood Forest or to Robin Hood but we have to bear in mind that the legend has grown apace over the years, hastened by the advent of film and television. Quite apart from whether Robin Hood existed at all or, if he did, whether he lived in Yorkshire and not Nottinghamshire, the notion of Sherwood Forest as continuous and extensive woodland is a false one. The royal forests, of which this was one, contained a high proportion of arable, pasture and common land, within which there would have been many large woods. Certainly few people in the Middle Ages would have lived beyond easy walking distance of thick woodland because of their need to rely upon it for fuel and food.

From Sherwood we continued to the Welbeck Estate through which Celia passed on her way north. Owing to a map reading error I strayed slightly from the correct track and ended up in ornamental driveways with wide mown grass verges lined with rhododendrons and large beech trees, the whole scene looked for all the world like the entrance to Windsor Great Park. I was convinced that I had made an error but could not work out how I had come to make it, with Cameron fidgeting while I was trying to study the map. After each day's ride I spend a long time studying my route on the map for the following day so that when I come to ride I reckon to be already quite well acquainted with the route. Several estate workers drove past and I was sure that someone would question my presence and put me right. Instead, however, they either raised their hats or waved and carried on their way. By that time I realised that I was well and truly lost and so I retraced my route to the entrance of the park and reoriented myself, what I had done was simply to enter the park half a mile too soon.

Celia describes Welbeck, now an army training college, as a house ''but old and low buildings but the parke is the noblest wood I ever saw, fine and stately''. What she does not mention is that Welbeck had in 1662 the first planned indoor riding school in the country. The Duke of Newcastle, the then owner of Welbeck, was the first exponent of classical riding in England. Classical riding had existed on the Continent for some time, and indeed it is still well known there today through such establishments as Vienna and Samur, but nothing was then known of it here and His Grace published a book on the subject and developed it in practice at the school. He was an exponent of the art of riding and of training with kindness and he was the inventor of the running or draw rein. He placed great reliance on it although he is depicted using a curb rein in most paintings; this is probably because for official portraits he would not want to have been seen using any artificial aids of this sort.

The Duke played a key role in improving British horses by importing horses from Italy and the Iberian peninsula and he described the Spanish Barb, which is a warm blooded horse originating in North Africa, as the gentlest of all horses. He was using Andalusians, Arabs and Barbs and also crossing them with native bred mares.

At the time of the Duke, riding meant in this country using the horse for transport, hunting or for social purposes and a great change had recently taken place in hunting as a result of the Civil War. Deer stocks had become depleted and so hunts had turned to the fox as a more readily available quarry. Such a fast straight moving animal called for lighter, faster hounds and, more importantly, for lighter and better bred horses which could gallop and jump. This in turn called for a different design of saddle with a lower pommel and a full flap: this hunting saddle became the envy of the riding world (and British saddlery still holds its own today). It has to be borne in mind that the enclosures had altered the whole face of the countryside and hunting over open moorland was becoming less common. It is against this background of the use of the horse for essentially practical purposes that one has to consider the work of the Duke of Newcastle in promoting riding for riding's sake. The notion of riding as an art had been hitherto unknown in this country.

Celia rode on from Welbeck and "...straight a mile thence is a fine pile of Buildings of stone very uniforme and high called Worsup Mannour...'' We crossed the route to Worksop Manor but it appeared from the map that we could not ride the mile long track which Celia rode. The Manor was indeed a very tall house and had the largest gallery of any house of the time, it was 212 feet long and 36 feet wide, when it was built in the mid 1580s. The galleries were used for ladies to take exercise when the weather was inclement and the second floor gallery had a continuous lantern of glass raised fifty feet above the Midland landscape. The Sixth Earl of Shrewsbury built the house as a very grand lodge rather than to accommodate full scale households. It was, however, destroyed by fire in 1761 and can now be gauged only from drawings and descriptions.

We backtracked on our route into Clumber Park, now owned by the National Trust, in order best to continue to Mansfield using bridleways as far as possible. Celia would have known nothing of the place as in her time all that was there was probably a hamlet, farms and perhaps a hunting lodge. The house was not built until 1767 and the gardens not laid out for another ten years. One of the principal attractions is the large river-like lake which at one time had a cascade as a feature and as I rode past I could see dredging work being carried out there. A century after Celia rode attempts were still being made to convert the heathland to agricultural use but it was not a success as the land kept reverting to its original state.

The main landscaping was done by William Gilpin, probably in the early nineteenth century, and he was responsible for the many terraces, parterre garden with ornamental vases, fountains and so on and also for the double lime avenue of trees, the longest tree-lined avenue in Europe. This avenue is so long that it is best viewed from the back of a horse or from an open horse-drawn carriage, for which it was indeed designed. I did not ride the whole length of it; I cut across country to the lake and rode along the well signed bridleways through the park in the lovely sunshine. At one point I was stopped by an employee of the Trust and asked whether I had a permit to ride. I responded that as I was on a bridleway one was not necessary. He accepted this and went on to offer help if I required it. The point was, however, again underlined that cross-country riders need to do their homework before setting out so that they can be sure that they are riding on the correct line.

I rode back into Sherwood Forest and headed southwards on mainly good going. Cameron was in high spirits and trotted along happily mile after mile for most of the day. He is a most comfortable horse to ride and has an easy trot which he can keep up for long periods.

I rode on through the Forest towards Mansfield and Nottingham; the Forest now is much smaller than in Celia's time and is owned by the Forestry Commission. I skirted Mansfield, a town that she obviously liked, being built of stone with a hospital for the elderly built by the Quakers where the inmates were given £8 a year each and a room and garden. It was here that she also noted that tammy, a type of woollen cloth used for linings and underwear (in those days at least), was made and dyed. By this stage I had joined up with where my route finished on the way north and from where I journeyed to Scarborough to make a fresh start heading south. I discovered that, despite my earlier frustrations in trying to get to Nottingham, I could have continued my way north from there after all. But no matter, I had completed the ride to date successfully and had done all that I had set out to do. I was very much looking forward to the next section through Derbyshire and I had decided to give Cameron a lift to the western side of the M1 as it would have been a very bitty sort of ride through industrial areas otherwise. Had he been a quieter horse I might have attempted it.

Elder Yard Chapel, Chesterfield

12

Gardens and Gardening

Celia was an enthusiast for the many gardens which she visited. A note about gardens as they existed before the seventeenth century may be appropriate before we go on to describe the visit to the splendid gardens at Chatsworth and Haddon Hall.

It is known that vegetable growing was carried on in Britain as far back as 5000 BC but the Romans were probably the first people to have gardens round their houses. They had elaborate designs of pools, fountains and quadrangles, each with individual gardens. The Romans were responsible for introducing numerous trees and plants to this country, as part of a process which has continued over thousands of years, and they cultivated a wide range of fruit and culinary vegatables including apples, vines and figs, fennel, leeks, onions, cabbages, cucumbers and asparagus.

With the departure of the Romans there followed, as in other fields, a gap in the art of gardening until medieval times. The monks were the earliest of the medieval gardeners; within the confines of the monastery they would commonly have herb gardens situated near the infirmary and their knowledge of the healing properties of herbs was extensive. They would also be self-sufficient in vegetables and flowers would be grown for the decoration of the altars. Fish would be reared in specially designed ponds, often made by damming a river.

Following the monks' gardens came castle gardens. Until then castle courtyards had been purely farmyards but with what we would now call a rise in the standard of living there came the creation of small ornamental gardens. From illustrated manuscripts one understands that these gardens generally consisted of a network of paths between which were raised beds planted with flowers. With the coming of the Tudors a period of great house building began and garden design, along with house design, started to become an art form. Many ideas were introduced from the Continent and this became a period of grand terraces, balustrades, flights of steps, topiary and other features. This was also the start of the knot garden, with low hedges of box or lavender arranged in lovers' knots or other geometric patterns, with between them planted flowers or herbs or sometimes simply gravel, not unlike the classical Japanese garden in fact. In late Tudor times books on plants and gardening began to appear, one of which was Gerard's "The Herbal" or "Generall Historie of Plantes". This richly illustrated encyclopedia included virtually all plants then known in Europe.

Moving closer to Celia's time, with the Stuarts came an increasing emphasis on scale and magnificence, with ideas again being imported from France and Italy. Courtiers became men of immense wealth and acquired vast tracts of land which they could afford to turn into parks and large gardens. Terraces, grand staircases, lakes and other water features all became increasingly popular and from this period it is possible to find detailed lists of ornamental plants in diaries and house accounts.

The Civil War brought about change and some of the large parks were lost; there was at the same time a growth of smaller gardens with the rise of a new class of minor gentry and yeomen. Two important books, both by the Rev William Lawson, came out in that period. One was called "A New Orchard and Garden" and the other "The Country House-Wife's Garden" - both became standard reading and were reprinted many times. They covered many aspects of the orchard and kitchen garden, summer flower gardens and even bee-keeping. A little later, towards the end of the seventeenth century, more gardening books and also seedsmen's and nurserymen's catalogues appeared and gardeners became keen to acquire rare and exotic plants. People also began to have garden plans drawn up and their gardens painted.

A further factor in the development of gardening was the Revolution of 1688 which brought William and Mary to the throne and with them new ideas: Hampton Court and Kensington Palace were the first two gardens to be changed under their influence against the background of the Dutch and French traditions of formal garden layouts, with parterres close to the house, horticultural areas to the sides and wilderness and orchards beyond. It was the beginning of this transition which Celia was witnessing as she rode around the country. She delighted in seeing new plants and ideas being implemented and in tasting new fruits such as strawberries and gooseberries. How curious it is that so many gardeners of today have so little knowledge of the historical background to their own gardens.

13

Chesterfield to Bakewell

With high hopes we entered Derbyshire and I spent that night in Chesterfield. Celia's first night in that county was similar to mine. She "lay here in a poor sorry inn, there was one good bed for us gentlewomen". If the hotel where I stayed had a good bed, it was certainly not in my room. I suffered as a result of the hard bed and was so stiff the next morning that I began to wonder whether I would be able to climb back on Cameron. He, however, had had a comfortable night a few miles up the road near Eckington, where Celia had stayed, and had been well looked after. The stables asked whether I would consider selling him as they were always looking for big middleweight horses but the answer of course was "no".

Everyone today knows of Chesterfield as the town whose parish church has a crooked spire, but Celia makes no mention of this feature. It is not known when the spire became crooked, probably as a result of the heat of the sun making the timbers of the spire tilt and bulge and it is possible that the now considerable distortion was less apparent in her time. In modern times the suburbs of the town have grown a great deal with the advent of coal mines, iron foundries and other industries but the names of many old streets survive such as Saltergate, Knifesmithgate and so on. The name Salter is found frequently throughout Derbyshire and it reminds one of the old trade routes along which salt was carried. The Unitarian chapel, built in 1694, was recently demolished; this is particularly sad as it was one of the oldest chapels in the country.

In the seventeenth century Chesterfield had a large number of shopkeepers, including grocers, chandlers, mercers, drapers and ironmongers. The craftsman's workshop formed another outlet for the retail trade, producing shoes, saddles, gloves, pots, pans and pewterware. There were also haberdasheries. There is still a street market with permanent stalls but everything had been packed away at the time of my visit in the evening. Celia comments that she bought herself two very good fat white pullets for 6d which in London would have cost 1/6 or 2/0.

As you leave Chesterfield the scenery changes dramatically with quiet roads and bridleways going up and down steep hills. Nearing Chatsworth there is a yet further change in scenery as the black peaty moor appears and one appreciates just how difficult travel in this area must have been three hundred years ago.

Chatsworth is the home of the Duke and Duchess of Devonshire. The title arose, by the way, as a result of a clerical error: it was intended that the name Derbyshire should have been used but the error having been made it could not be altered. Celia saiys that ''...all Derbyshire is full of steep hills, and nothing but the peakes of hills as thick one by another is seen in most of the County which are very steepe which makes travelling tedious, and the miles long, you see neither hedge nor tree but only low drye stone walls round some ground, else it is only hills and dales as thick as you can imagine, but tho' the surface of the earth looks barren yet those hills are impregnated with rich Marbles, Stones, Metals, Iron and Copper and coale mines in their bowells, from whence we may see the wisdom and its benignitye of our greate Creator to make up the defficiency of a place by an equivolent as also the diversity of the creation which increaseth its Beauty''.

Defoe also described Chatsworth as situated in the most inhospitable place on earth and one wonders if he was not right. Certainly as I approached the estate the black, peaty and barren moors stood out. As I was to find out, the rate of progress was very slow and in accounts of various routes and rides around Derbyshire hills it was stated that one could not better one or two miles to the hour; with the time spent doing the necessary map reading I doubt whether our progress was above two and a half miles an hour.

I had been given permission to ride through the Chatsworth estate and was delighted to find one of the estate workers in his van waiting for me at the edge of Beeley Moor. I apologised for being a little late and for requiring him to be working on a Saturday morning for my benefit. His retort was that if he had not been helping me he would have been shopping with his wife. His main concern was that I should take my time riding through the park so that I could enjoy the scenery to the full.

Gates were unlocked for me and I was escorted across the wild moor which, despite a misty haze, offered the most beautiful and expansive views. There was an important added bonus for me in that I was relieved of the burden of map-reading for a while. We trotted uphill for some distance and then after a while dropped down into the park. Our arrival startled the deer and caused them to scatter in all directions, jumping as they went, and Cameron wanted to copy them. Luckily for me, however, he contained himself and we trotted steadily across the grass of the park until we were met at the edge of the pinetum by two young horticulturists from the estate. We negotiated a small wooden bridge and a narrow gate and I felt very privileged to ride through the gardens which cover a hundred acres.

My first view was of the Victorian plantation designed by Paxton. It was in this area that some work was being carried out in 1985 when a statue was accidentally dislodged from its plinth. It transpired that the statue could have been Elizabethan, certainly the present Duke who has lived in the house for forty years had not seen it before. We then passed the simple grotto which was originally thatched but now has a bandstand built above it. The interior of the grotto is lined with minerals and shining crystals of copper salts; Celia would not have seen the grotto, however, as this feature began to appear in gardens a century after her time. There are some ancient oaks near the grotto and near the park, these were originally part of the northern end of Sherwood Forest remarkable as that may seem. Opposite the grotto is the grotto lake or pond which is an old fish pond, one of the sources of food in the seventeenth and eighteenth centuries.

The present Duchess is keen on conservation and this was evident from the fact that along our route were many wild flowers which had been allowed to flourish. I rode just above the cascade, the elaborate complex of fountains and waterfalls which was finished in 1696 and so was brand new at the time of Celia's visit. She was very impressed with the gardens just as I was three centuries later. In her time there were three ornamental gardens. One she describes as containing many stone and brass statues. Statues in gardens became popular in Elizabethan times; many represented Elizabeth who was linked to the goddess Diana in the popular imagination and the vogue was said to be connected with the change of the national religion from Roman Catholicism to Protestantism. Celia would also have seen the famous fountains with sea horses which are there today, still full of life and movement. The original material was marble but some of the statuary was replaced in the nineteenth century by ordinary building stone. Another remarkable fountain is the one which looks like a willow tree which was constructed in 1692; in winter it looks much like a leafless tree, but it is made from copper and lead and an unwary passerby can trip a valve which transforms the "tree" into a fountain. The various Dukes and their families over the years took great delight in playing with this toy and soaking their visitors.

It is likely that, although she does not mention it, Celia would have seen the Duke's greenhouse. The accounts for 1698 show that fifty orange, twenty six apricot and fourteen peach trees were purchased from a nursery in Brompton Park, an indication of the way in which owners of gardens were seeking out the exotic at that time. Sadly, a hundred years after Celia's visit Capability Brown swept away many of the formal gardens, parterres and terraces and radically altered the gardens.

We then descended a steep and narrow zigzag path to beyond the kitchen garden and then to the front of the house. The last hour had without question been the highlight of the whole trip. When I started out to ride through the garden I had been a little apprehensive of what Cameron's reaction might have been. He has been known to munch flowers and spook at statues or the like and my husband had been whistling snatches of the song ''Where have all the flowers gone?''. However, Cameron behaved impeccably and I need not have worried. I bade my guide farewell and thanked her for all her help. She was a student doing her practical work before going on to horticultural college and made it clear that she loved being at Chatsworth. She said that it was like being in one large happy family.

We emerged into the car park and found ourselves in a different world. Visitors from many countries crowded around and Cameron became one of the tourist attractions as he had at Newby Hall. People were wanting to be photographed with him and plied me with questions about where we had been, what we were doing, how far we were going and so on.

Later, with Cameron safely stabled on the estate, I visited the house and gardens as an ordinary tourist and was thrilled by the literally weeping willow tree, the cascade and the many treasures in the house. It was a hot day and people were walking barefoot up the cascade; I just could not imagine what Celia would have made of this, even though the grounds have always been open to visitors.

The first house at Chatsworth was built by ''Bess of Hardwick'', the work starting in 1552. The site at that time was prone to flooding and had difficult access across the moors to the east. The original house was the square block that one sees today; few alterations were made at Chatsworth until the end of the seventeenth century. In 1686, eleven years before Celia visited, the First Duke began by pulling down part of the South Front. The story is that he intended only to alter this part of the house, but he so enjoyed this work that he didn't know when to stop! The East Front followed and then new outbuildings. George London and Henry Wise designed a formal garden and a Frenchman, Grillet, the cascade. Chatsworth was said to be perfect in the geometry of the large country house ''parterre'' (an arrangement of flower beds with knot gardens, topiary and statues). Records show that Talman's south front measures 473ft by 227ft; the contract states explicitly how each quarter should be laid out ''with borders of good Earth fit to receave such a Collection of Hardy Ever-greens and flowering trees, Shrubs and flowers......'' There was also a bowling green and pavilion.

Celia said that ''the Duke's house lyes just at the foote of this steepe hill which is like a precipice just at the last, notwithstanding the Dukes house stands on a little riseing ground from the River Derwent which runs all along the front of the house and by a little fall made in the water which makes a pretty murmurring noise; before the gate there is a large Parke and severall fine gardens one without another with gravell walkes and squairs of grass with stone statues in them and in the middle of each garden''. This description can hardly be bettered today, but what would surprise Celia if she were to return now would be the crowds of people from many countries eager to enter the house and gardens to enjoy them just as she did.

The Cascade, Chatsworth

From Chatsworth Celia visited Bakewell but I decided to ride across the park and up the steep hill opposite the house, over the top and down to Haddon Hall. I was expected there that afternoon and so had to defer my visit to the town. From Chatsworth I made my way over the River Derwent to the unfenced public road which goes through the park. The park was full of sheep with a few cattle and there was a constant stream of vehicles on the road. We crossed the open country away from the house but still within the park, climbing the steep hill but stopping frequently to gaze back at Chatsworth. I was treated to a view which was quite unforgettable. The house, set against the backdrop of wooded hills, appeared timeless and utterly perfect.

On reaching the top of the hill, with Cameron blowing slightly, it took me a few minutes to sort out how to enter the wood but eventually I decided that we were on the right path to Haddon Hall. I made my way through the wood to be greeted when I emerged by the sight of a steep descent across an open field, so steep that I could never have stayed on Cameron mounted. I dismounted and led him in a series of slides and hops, remounting at the foot of the hill but only to find that we had to climb to the top of another ridge. As we progressed up a partially hollowed way cattle stared down at us, but Cameron was by now taking far less notice of the presence of cattle and sheep close by than he used. If, however, they had galloped across with their tails up I had no doubt that he would have taken off or bucked me off.

The next two gates had an impossibly difficult arrangement for riders in that they were linked together by chains and poles so that they would shut after one had gone through. However, it was impossible to go through mounted; it was a struggle to get the gate open wide enough to get Cameron through before it snapped shut, a lethal arrangement for horses as they could very easily be hipped (damage to the hips which can be caused by a glancing blow going through a narrow gateway and which can be irremediable).

The next descent - would we never arrive at Haddon? - was a zigzag which reminded me of the hanger above Selborne in Hampshire where Gilbert White lived and worked. To cap it all the going was very slippery after overnight rain and progress was slow but, mercifully, safe. Cameron soon found that the easiest way to navigate steep, wet slopes was to go down with his forelegs moving normally but with his hind legs held close together. So he went down in a controlled slide almost as if on skis - it must have looked comical but it worked. The whole episode was an interesting example of how quickly an intelligent horse can learn how to cope with different terrain and difficult situations.

At last we found ourselves approaching the back of Haddon Hall, one of the seats of the Duke of Rutland, where we were met by the staff who had been expecting us and had indeed been out looking for us for some time as we had taken much longer than expected. We were made most welcome and I dismounted, left Cameron with Bill who had arrived with the backup transport, and went off on a tour of inspection. While I visited the house, Cameron made the most of his opportunity to crop the grass by the River Wye, one of the three main rivers of Derbyshire. Horses love to eat fresh grass and stopping frequently to allow them to graze will keep them going, however long the journey.

Celia describes the place as "...a good old house, all built of stone on a hill but nothing very curious as the mode now is, there is a large Parke upon a great ascent from the house, which is built around a Court, the Parke is one part of some of the highest hills which gives a great prospect all over the Country - but indeed all Darbyshire is but a world of peaked hills which from some of the highest you discover the rest like steeples or tops of hills as thick as can be, and tho' they appear so close yet the steepness down and up takes up the time that you go it, as if so many miles, and were on the ground, measur'd would be in length as much as miles on a plaine". She was obviously less keen on Haddon than on Chatsworth but the two have to be viewed as utterly different. Chatsworth is a formal creation, and indeed a magnificent and breathtaking one, but Haddon is a medieval house which has changed little with the passage of time. One sees it today as Celia would have done, with its painted ceilings, wall paintings in the chapel and set amidst surroundings which appear to have been created by Nature herself.

Haddon Hall

The gardens do not have the formality of Chatsworth but are laid out in a series of stone walled terraces which were created in the early seventeenth century, but a few decades before Celia's arrival. The Ninth Duke planned the restoration to recreate the gardens as she would have seen them: the total effect is quite delightful. I was fortunate enough to see the gardens when the roses were in full bloom and the effect was spectacular.

It is interesting to note that Haddon Hall's accounts from the mid 1500s have been kept and give some indication of supplies purchased and of how the occupants lived. They used several different sources for groceries, including local markets, fairs, urban shops and hawkers ; surprisingly, few items were purchased in nearby Bakewell. Exotic groceries often appeared in the accounts: from Chesterfield they would obtain hops, spices, wines and sugar; these would be transported over the difficult East Moor. They also purchased veal, mustard, malt and all kinds of fish. Whether these goods came overland from London or from the coast is not known. The spices included ginger, nutmeg, cloves and mace, and the fish oysters, mussels, eels, pike and white herring. A few years after Celia Fiennes, Defoe saw fish being transported alive in great butts on waggons and this is still done in Central Europe. It is also recorded that a horse load of pears and quinces was bought, probably from a hawker.

Eventually I took my leave and boxed Cameron back to Chatsworth for the night. After settling him in and giving instructions about his food I left him in capable hands and went on into Bakewell. I unhesitatingly award these stables the equestrian five star. It was evident that he appreciated them as, when the owner checked him last thing at night, she found him completely stretched out flat and fast asleep. It is most unusual for a horse to sleep in this way in strange stables; the usual way is to remain with legs curled underneath like a dog, remaining alert for any possible danger which might arise.

As I approached Bakewell the weather changed dramatically. The heavens opened and rain came down like stair-rods. Water was pouring down the gutters of the steep roads as I arrived at the night's lodging and I found myself standing on the doorstep, soaking wet and holding my equally wet tack. Eventually I got inside but even then it was not easy to struggle off my riding boots and get my belongings and tack under cover. At last I was drying off in a comfortable room with coffee to help restore my flagging spirits. Having had a bath and become human again we descended the steep hill into Bakewell and found an excellent restaurant which helped complete the process of restoration.

14

Bakewell to Buxton

Next day I collected Cameron from the stables, mounted him and set out to follow the same route as Celia would have ridden from Edensor, the village by Chatsworth, pronounced Ensor. Cameron, well rested, was very full of himself and I was struggling with the gate which leads into Edensor village when a kind motor cyclist told me to sit still while he did it for me. This was a great help and was much appreciated. Safely through, I was delighted to find that the road is still in existence and not even completely metalled. We went on through the village at a spanking trot and, still trotting, climbed the steep hill towards Ball Cross. It was quite exciting, at the next road junction, to find an old guide stoop which was erected in 1709 just after Celia's visit.

I decided to take a short cut through Manners Wood on a bridleway to save mileage; after riding for some while, however, I was convinced that I had missed my turning. I was not at all sure of the way and asked a walker whom I met who told me, wrongly as it turned out, that I was on a footpath leading to the golf course and the bridleway was farther into the wood. Shortly I found the way barred by a fallen tree: there was no way round and it was a question of dismounting and seeing whether Cameron could wriggle his way through the hazard. He is remarkably agile for a big horse and, sure enough, he got past the obstacle without any fuss. After riding for a few more minutes I realised that we really were lost and must be approaching the bridleway to Haddon, in quite the wrong direction.

We had to retrace our steps and I began to wonder whether I would be able to get Cameron past the tree for a second time. After dismounting I saw to my horror that one of his hooves had gone over the edge the first time round at a point where there is a drop of a hundred feet or so. We did manage to negotiate the tree again, missed the correct bridleway completely and rode back to the metalled road, thence descending into Bakewell. My journey had been hazardous enough but in Celia's time the route would have appeared almost impossible to travellers on horseback. Remember that maps were virtually non-existent and guides were essential for strangers to the area.

Bakewell gives the appearance of lying on low ground because of the surrounding hills, but in fact it is about 400 feet above sea level. It has a prosperous air, one indication of which was the ease with which a suitable place to eat could be found. The town had a market charter as far back as 1200 and the market thrived as other markets were quite distant and in Defoe's time people would travel in as far as twelve or fifteen miles. The town has much older origins, it is mentioned in Domesday and there is an imposing Saxon cross in the churchyard which probably predates the town by a century. The town also had a brief period as a spa, but it was on trade that the place was built up. The bath house was built in 1697 at just about the time of Celia's visit but she either missed it or did not think it of sufficient importance to mention. The packhorse bridge was built in 1694, just before her visit but she does not mention that either. She does, however, mention the number of nonconformist meetings in the town and she travelled to villages around to hear various preachers. If there were early chapels in and around Bakewell they have not survived as there is no mention of any in a recent compilation of chapels in Derbyshire.

The appearance of the town centre has probably altered little since Celia's time, with the splendid fourteenth century bridge over the River Wye and the old market hill. What has altered, however, is that the town is now choc a bloc with tourists in the season; indeed I was told that as many as forty thousand people can descend on the place at any one time. She described it as "a neate market town, it stands on a hill yet you descend a vast hill to it, which you would thinke impossible to go down and we were forced to fetch a great compass, and by reason of the steepness and hazard of the Wayes - if you take a wrong way there is no passing - you are forced to have Guides as in all parts of Darbyshire ... they of the country will climbe up and down with their horses those steep precipices".

The name Bakewell has, of course, passed into the language because of the famous tart or pudding as it is called locally, which arose from a culinary accident in the Rutland Arms in the Square. I made a point of buying a Bakewell pudding which had a somewhat rough and unprepossessing appearance. It was, however, quite delicious and served as a lunchtime snack for the next couple of days. It is nothing at all like a Bakewell tart, although they can be bought as well. The pudding is like an almond flavoured egg custard on a bed of jam and is filling as well as good to eat.

Instead of using the bridleways going north from Bakewell as planned I decided to use the Monsal Trail which is open to horse riders. It follows the route of the old railway line which passed through the town but the choice of route turned out to be a mixed blessing. I followed the trail as far as I could, trotting most of the way to make up for lost time, but there was no way off for horses at Monsal Head where the old tunnel is closed and walkers have to find there way round over stiles. We had to retrace our steps to south of Great

Longstone, but the gradients were gentle and it was easy going. Our way took us northwards through Rowland and up the very steep bridleway to High Rake, with its disused mineshafts and open cast workings. Cameron negotiated these steep climbs with ease and he was obviously extremely fit. The views of the White Peak area, the limestone region as opposed to the millstone grit of the Black Peak area, which the route afforded were really quite exceptional. The word "rake", by the way, is encountered frequently in the area. It is a northern dialect word which means route or path and does not appear to be connected with the racking gate of horses as has been suggested. There is, however, another use of the term to describe a long outcrop of ore and the word is used in a non-dialect sense to describe a line of railway coaches connected together.

If it had been a working day the ride would have been made hazardous by the presence of large earth-moving machines, tractors and bulldozers which stood idle near the road. Our route swung off westward and a treat was in store, as for the next mile or so we had a wide green track to follow bounded by stone walls, rather like Dere Street in Scotland, with marvellous views around. I was enjoying myself so much that I did not take the opportunity of a good canter or gallop which presented itself. At the end we turned northwards and climbed again. At the summit I opted out of the steep descent to Darlton Quarry and instead went westward to Houseley, joining an old unmetalled road to Eyam. This road was full of interest as it led past little fields, each of about half an acre and each bounded by drystone walls, and entered the village at Townhead.

Eyam is the plague village but it appeared as any other and although reminders of its history exist they have to be sought out. In fields behind the village, with dairy cows grazing around, there are various graves of plague victims. I also visited Mompesson's Well which was a handover point for food and money, the villagers leaving coins covered with vinegar to guard against the transfer of infection. Unfortunately, the church where the guides to the village could be obtained closed at 4pm and I arrived too late, having ridden for a good deal of the day. My tour of the village was therefore less well informed than I would have liked. Thirty years before Celia's visit to Derbyshire the infection was apparently brought to the village in a box of clothes sent to the village tailor from London. Some 250 of the 350 inhabitants died in the course of the next few months but everyone steadfastly refused to leave the village. The rector, William Mompesson, and the recently ejected nonconformist minister, Thomas Stanley, continued to look after their flocks and to maintain them in their decision to stay put. The infection lasted for some fifteen months.

I had been looking forward to tackling the next stretch out of Eyam but I was advised not to ride Cameron over the very steep hills to Castleton and Mam Tor because of the risk of stifle injury in a horse used mainly in the lowlands.

Later I regretted this decision as he was extremely fit and could trot up 1 in 5 hills with no problems at all. So I visited both places without him.

Celia commented in some detail about her visit to the area. She saw Mam Tor as I did, as a dramatic peak with expansive wild views all around. The reason for its choice as a site for a hill fort by Bronze Age man was evident. Enthusiastic walkers were much in evidence on the occasion of my visit but in Celia's time it must have been a very lonely place indeed. One could look over the Vale of Edale and the associated valleys, with in the distance Kinder Scout and the beginning of the Pennine Way. She described Mam Tor as a high hill which is completely round, except on the Castleton side where it looks as if it has been cut like an old-fashioned hay rick. The reason is that Mam Tor, or the shivering mountain as it is known, sheds sand, shale and gritstone after frost or heavy rain.

At the same time, I briefly visited Castleton the small town close by which is now packed with tourists at holiday times. One can see why Celia commented on the exceedingly steep hill which could not be descended by foot or horse, the road zigzagging at least three or four times in the course of the descent. The caves can still be visited but whereas a man used to live by begging to show visitors the caves the whole thing is now highly commercialised.

In Celia's time there were problems in navigating through Derbyshire and even today those problems have not all been resolved. In the late seventeenth and early eighteenth centuries the custom was to erect guide stoops or stones across open moorland, sometimes with direction arrows and mileages on them. This was the beginning of the system of signposting which we accept as normal today in even the most remote places. Cairns were also put up to help people on their way and guides were available to be employed by travellers: sometimes the use of a guide was essential, especially in severe winter weather. One has to remember that the only maps available in Celia's time were those produced by John Ogilby in 1675 which were not sufficiently detailed to be of real use; they were designed to be studied at home rather than on the back of a horse. According to W B Crump, the earliest reference in English literature to a traveller consulting a map is in "Pilgrim's Progress" when Greatheart was guiding Christina and her family through the enchanted ground. From the passage, it appears that Bunyan was referring to Ogilby's maps.

There are many stories of people getting lost in winter and freezing to death. Strangers were not the only people to fear the moors. A nonconformist parson and apothecary from Chapel-en-le-Frith in Derbyshire, the Rev James Clegg, set out for Crich in winter and wrote later of his journey "... a kind Providence directed me safely over the east moor and I got in in good time...'' His diary however records accidents on other journeys. In March 1730 he narrowly escaped a dangerous fall when his mare jumped into a stone pit in the dark. On an earlier journey, visiting his parents in Rockdale in 1723, he found on his return that the snow was thawing quickly and the waters rising fast. He and his mare were swept downstream from a ford of which he wrote "... thro' the mercy of God I continued to sit her and with much struggling got her through the river...'' Another person who had a similarly distressing experience was Adam Eyre of Hazledene Hall also in Derbyshire; he survived and also gave thanks for his deliverance. On another occasion the same Adam Eyre gave two pence to a guide to see him safely home even though he was only ten miles distant.

The name Eyre which Charlotte Bronte used for her novel Jane Eyre originated in Hathersage in Derbyshire, the book being set in the locality and places can be recognised. I did stay at Highlow Hall which was one of the Eyre halls, high up on the moors with beautiful views all around and with scarcely another house in sight.

There are entries in the burial registers of Penistone in Yorkshire of people who lost their lives through imprudence in not seeking the help of guides in bad weather conditions. On 10 March 1775 William Wordsworth, not the poet, starved to death on the moors. On 15 February 1763 J Charlesworth from Burton was recorded as lost in snow. On 6 March 1764 James Marsh starved in the snow. These records are the tip of an iceberg of death and injury which bring home to us how desperately dangerous travel in winter was in Celia Fiennes' time.

I also visited Tideswell which gets its name from the ebbing and flowing well which used to be there. I tried to track down the site of the well which Celia visited and an old man in a cafe was delighted to give me directions. It was with a sense of excitement that I approached what appeared to be a rockery in the garden of a house on the outskirts of the village but was in fact the site of the old well. The spring would rise and fall several times an hour but it ceased to function about a hundred years ago. Tideswell was at one time an area where the kings of England would hunt, travelling there from Sherwood Forest via Dronfield. This route was a circuitous one but was possibly chosen to avoid the very steep ways. Unfortunately I discovered later that the well which Celia visited was almost certainly at Barmoor Clough, some miles away, the sort of error which is an occupational hazard for anyone who seeks to follow the footsteps of history. I did take the trouble to seek out the correct well and was thrilled to find it still there alongside a busy road. It is close to Elden Hole and so one can plot with fair certainty the route which Celia took.

The limestone structure of Derbyshire quickly soaks up surface water and this led in ancient times to its veneration. Wells were dressed as an invocation to the gods or water spirits. In a familiar pattern, this practice became a Christian one and today well dressing ceremonies are held in various villages in Derbyshire. I visited Stoney Middleton and was quite amazed by the beauty of the pictures of petals and leaves stuck to clay which were erected at the sites of wells or on the banks of streams. The subjects varied but in the main related to bible stories. It is difficult to do justice to the beauty of the pictures or to the amount of work which had gone into them. It has been suggested that spas were a secularisation of this water worship. People came to believe that substances in the water did them good and what might be called pilgrimages were made to the spas for a form of water worship to be carried out.

Having much enjoyed this fascinating area, I remounted Cameron and headed on towards Buxton and the next night's stabling.

17th C mining

15

Buxton to Ashbourne

When I arrived in Buxton I recalled that Celia had commented on the difficulty of finding the town; in her time it was impossible, owing to the steepness and narrowness of the ways, for coaches or waggons to pass and the landscape was barren, with no trees or hedges and only drystone walls to form enclosures. She also comments that nine miles took six hours' going. Even today on horseback one's progress is probably not much above two miles an hour. In her time people were going to Buxton for the baths and there were large entertaining houses or hotels for visitors. A hundred years after Celia's visit St Ann's Crescent was built and behind it stables and a riding school for up to a hundred horses. This gives an indication of how prosperous the place became. But change has been inevitable and, sadly, the riding school has now been converted into the Devonshire Hospital.

The town still has a prosperous and distinctive air and trees, gardens and parks abound. However, it was no time for enjoyment as the weather had changed dramatically and July had become more like October or November. A gale was blowing and rain was sweeping across the valleys as I made my way to the night's lodging outside Buxton, just over the county boundary in Staffordshire. I had booked Cameron into a riding centre but he did not settle because of the howling gale, which might have reminded him of the 1987 hurricane which devastated a large part of the south and east of England. Unfortunately he panicked slightly and as a result lost his front shoe again but I was told that it could be replaced in the morning and this encouraged me somewhat. I was surprised that I had to provide my own hay but this was because the previous year's crop had been completely ruined and the present year's was still uncut. I gathered that a great deal of the land thereabouts is too poor even to yield a hay crop; it is a forbidding area where existence is clearly much harder than in the south.

Having sorted out Cameron and settled and fed him, I went to the inn where I had booked but found to my chagrin that the room had been let because of some confusion. This turned out to be no bad thing as alternative accommodation was found in a farmhouse nearby. But my troubles were not yet over as my hostess had been away for some time and, although she made me very welcome, she could not have realised that the bed was damp. I put on my sweater and trousers as protection and spent an uncomfortable night but the next morning a magnificent breakfast went a long way to help me recover my spirits and get me back on the road.

The whole episode reminded me of Celia's experiences in Buxton, where she found that the meals were expensive but the room was included in the price. The bedrooms, however, were bad and furthermore might contain as many as four beds. If one did not have enough company of one's own, more people would be added so one could be sharing not only the room but the very bed with strangers. Celia stayed there however for two nights, much against her will, as one of her servants was ill.

When I got to the stables it was apparent that Cameron had spent a miserable night too: his coat was staring and he looked somewhat out of sorts. With the howling wind and rain, coupled with a draughty stable, he would have been happier with a rug on. However we both survived the experience.

My route then took me southwards to Ashbourne on the Tissington Trail which is an old railway track and I was a little concerned that I would spend a good deal of my time riding in cuttings as in East Anglia. Although such a route is pleasant riding one sees very little. However, my fears were not realised and I found myself riding on a ridge for a great deal of the way which commanded pleasant, if windswept, views. The going consisted of grass and cinders and we tried to keep up a steady trot for most of the way. However, there were great numbers of cyclists and walkers to contend with and at times it was slightly hazardous to keep going at all. The thought is always at the back of my mind that Cameron might take it into his head under such circumstances to buck or kick out at what he no doubt sees as a potential threat. But again all was well and he behaved impeccably. The weather had improved slightly but we were now on lower ground, although from time to time I was soaked by squally showers. Poor Cameron, going sideways to avoid the sting of the heavy rain, was clearly eager to finish for the day. Although we had had a bad day of it, I had to bear in mind that this was only the third time that we had been really soaked in riding the whole Northern Journey of Celia Fiennes.

The Tissington Trail, which is about 18 miles long, joins up with the High Peak Trail and is rightly a popular route with cyclists. However the old gate problem again arose and for the first few miles there were many to open and close, some of which had the habit of blowing open just as one was about to fasten them or of blowing closed when riding through. Later though this problem disappeared. I was surprised to find no other horse riders on the Trail, but perhaps they knew to keep away at weekends because of all the cyclists using it.

We paused for a break at the village of Tissington, a picture book place in a park like situation with a long tradition of well dressing. There are five wells still; it is not known when they were first dressed but the custom certainly dates back to pagan times. It is generally supposed that there was a Christian revival of the custom after the Black Death, probably around 1349, when it was thought that the pure water supply was the reason for the complete absence of the infection around Tissington. After a few more miles of the Trail we arrived at Ashbourne; I was conscious that we were all the time making our way southwards as the dramatic scenery of the Peak District had given way to a hilly but more pastoral landscape.

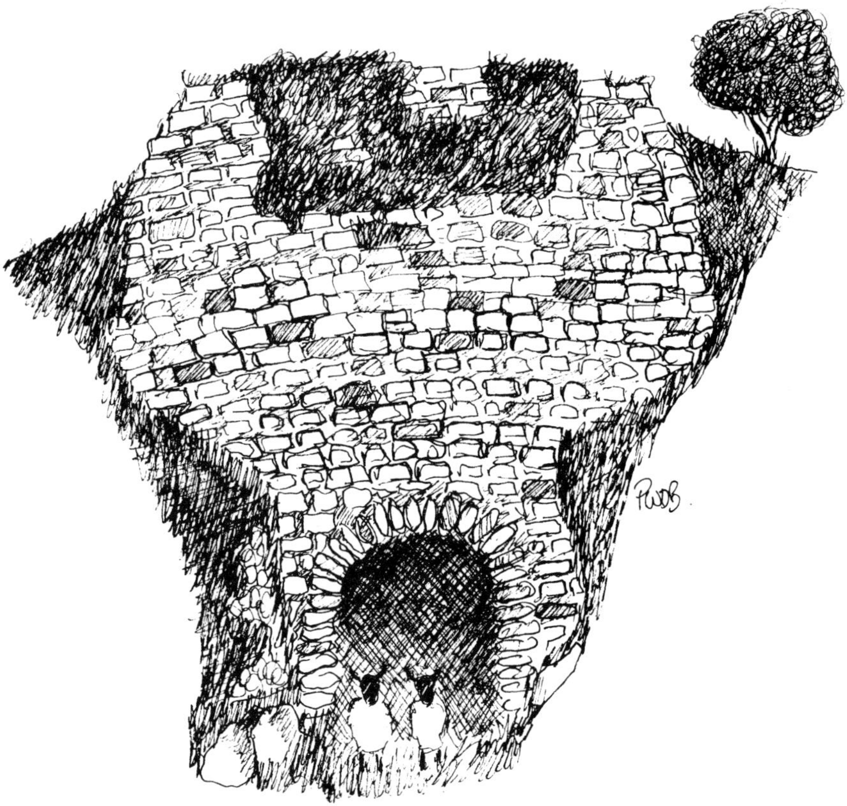

Lime kiln, Derbyshire

16

Ashbourne to Warwick

Ashbourne is known as the Gateway to the Peak and is also now famous as a source of bottled mineral water. The town is surrounded by hills and lies in a valley. Celia found that the lower Dove valley was full of enclosures as indeed it still is, an area of cattle, sheep and stone walls but without the moorland. Dr Johnson and Boswell stayed in the town at The Green Man Hotel, a name with ancient associations which appears to link with the practice of well dressing and one of the very few hostelries left in the country with an inn sign over the roadway. I was, of course, in Dr Johnson country as his father came from Great Cubley between Ashbourne and Sudbury and it was in Uttoxeter market that the great man performed his famous penance for refusing to help his father with his bookstall there.

Celia went on towards Uttoxeter, visiting on the way, according to her journal, the copper mines at Snelston which were in operation from an early date, although modern scholarship doubts whether copper was ever known in the area. From Snelston her route would have taken her across the River Dove at the Hanging Bridge at Mayfield, an important river crossing since medieval times, and then along the route of the present-day road to Uttoxeter. She makes reference to ''...a very exact House and Gardens of one Mr Cotten a Justice of Peace''. This was not Beresford Hall as suggested in the notes to the modern edition of the Journeys; that house had belonged to Charles Cotton the poet but he had been dead ten years at the time of her visit and the house sold out of the family. It is almost certain that the house in question was Crakemarsh Hall, two miles from Uttoxeter.

Instead of riding directly to Uttoxeter, as there were few bridleways I rode in a more easterly direction through the villages and parks of Osmaston and Shirley and southwards to Longford which afforded some good tracks through pleasing hilly scenery. I was enjoying the riding in lovely sunshine but near Longford I again encountered gates which could not be opened from Cameron's back, so I ended up by leading him rather than repeatedly dismounting and remounting which I find such an effort. If he were smaller and I had more spring it would be a different story.

We were now riding in the area of Derbyshire which Celia visited on her Great Journey in 1698. We passed briefly through Uttoxeter and made our way into

Staffordshire where the soil structure changes to sand and gravel with some clay. In Celia's time it was well wooded but today only a few woods remain.

Cameron was stabled that night at Ingestre Hall at the edge of the Chase, which was another house visited by Celia. The stables were large, grand and old and were ranged around a cobbled courtyard; each box was of a good size and was complete with what were obviously the original fittings, with a passage running in front in the usual fashion of those times. Cameron could well have been in the very same stable which her horse had used. He settled down well as he always does, paying little attention to all the activity of what is now a busy riding centre.

The fine house probably looks much as it did in her time, with large bow windows running up the whole front of the building so that one's immediate impression is of a house full of windows. The gardens are more informal now and the house is used as an arts centre. The church is attributed to Sir Christopher Wren and was newly built at the time of Celia Fiennes. Its remote situation does not prepare one for a city type church in the familiar classical style of Wren. Brick was used in this area early on, apparently because of a lack of other materials. The whole place was altogether delightful to visit as the sense of the past was quite tangible.

Celia comments on the presence of conifers in the grounds of the house which were unusual at that time. They were reintroduced, along with sycamores, in the seventeenth century and she was struck by the way that they kept their leaves. Defoe also comments, some thirty years later, that Ingestre had the "...finest park and gardens in all this part of England". That was before the remodelling carried out by Lancelot (Capability) Brown.

Close by, certainly within five miles, is Wolseley which was the home of one of Celia's relations. It stands in a park by the A51, the Stafford to Rugby road, with the River Trent flowing through the grounds. The gardens had, at the time of my visit, just been opened to the public and one can now enjoy them as Celia and her mother did. The gardens are well described in Celia's journal, as having both gravel and green walks, with the River Trent running by. There were many small trees and honeysuckle plants and a great deal of fruit was grown. She mentions fruit trees, including apples, pears and cherries, and soft fruit such as strawberries: these were like buttons and were from a second crop. There were fine flowers also, including white and yellow tuber roses. Celia stayed here, sometimes for as long as several weeks, on a number of her journeys. She did, unusually, make excurions by coach and would probably have used the equipage belonging to the house. The house was newly built and was surrounded by a moat, with a fine courtyard and gatehouse and a large deer park, containing both red and fallow deer, which was used for hunting. The park was six miles round and included woodland; it can be assumed that it also included part of Cannock Chase.

From Ingestre I rode south and into the Chase in warm sunshine, trotting in places but for part of the way the track was very stony and we were reduced to a walk. I visited some of the sites which Celia had visited during her time at Wolseley in the course of her Great Journey and of other separate trips. The going in the main was easy but across the Chase were many notices warning one not to stray from the track because of the danger of subsidence as a result of coal mining, which was already being carried on there in Celia's time. "...not farre from hence they have mines of the fine sort of Coale, that is hard and will be pollish'd like black marble, for salt or boxes or the such like, the only difference it will not bear the fire as marble does else it resembles it very much; there were of these mines just by, but now they have come to the end of this veine and so there is none within six or seven miles; this is the Pitt Coale that cloven and burns like a candle and it makes white ashes like the Scotch-Coale.."

Celia also comments that a load purchased for three or four shillings would give a poor family warmth for the whole winter. My image of the Chase had been of a wild and desolate place but it turned out to be neither of those. It had wooded areas interspersed with open valleys with streams in them: the only thing to spoil my pleasure was a sudden abundance of flies which bothered Cameron considerably. From Celia's comments the area has changed little; she complains how the ferns and brackens would overrun the grass and would be cut and burnt in heaps each year. She also makes reference to the wild oak trees and wild fruit such as bilberries, and to hawking being carried on there.

I passed Tixall on my way southwards, together with Haywood Park and Penkridge Bank. These were both gentlemen's estates visited by Celia but they are now swallowed up as part of the Forestry Commission holding in the area. I rode on but at the end of a track known as The Marquis Drive was disconcerted to find that the gate of a level crossing was padlocked shut. This created a serious problem as the way round was along busy roads. Indeed every road in the area, even small side roads, carried fast, heavy traffic screaming round the bends. Tyre squeal is a sound which has long since disappeared elsewhere and it was most curious, if not disturbing, to hear it again. There was nothing for it but to grit my teeth and brave the narrow, twisty and busy road for about a mile. This I did without mishap and then I was relieved that we could re-enter the safety of the forest.

I rode through it for about a mile and then found myself on a golf course with tracks going off in every direction. I became slightly disoriented and it was difficult to read my map with Cameron fidgeting and jumping like a two year old every time he spied a golf bag or a ball being hit. After riding for some twenty minutes I realised that I had gone in completely the wrong direction, there was nothing for it but to retrace our steps back to the golf course and start again. I struck off towards Beaudesert Old Park which is now Forestry Commission land and went on to Cannock Wood, the nearest point to Lichfield to which I intended riding. Sadly the only remaining sign of the Beaudesert estate, which was at one time noted for its fine gardens and park, was some artificial lakes which I chanced upon. Celia had noted that coal was being mined within the park and drawn up in baskets with a little wheel or windlass as might be found on a well and much of the area around is owned by British Coal today.

Lichfield was already a thriving place in Celia's time and indeed had been so since the Middle Ages. She comments on the good houses, which were being built from local brick. It was a place favoured by gentlemen and society generally to live in and its location, situated close to the main roads going north, helped its growth.

I did not ride through this area as it is so heavily built up with few bridleways, so I boxed Cameron on to beyond Warwick. If he had been completely traffic-proof I would have attempted to ride this stretch but opted for safety and peace of mind.

17

Warwick to Great Horwood

When Celia visited Warwick it was being rebuilt following a disastrous fire four or five years earlier. The place is, as a result, one of the best surviving examples of a brick-built town of the time of William and Mary. The Commissioners who were supervising the work insisted that the High Street and Jury Street be widened and straightened and that the houses be built of two or three storeys, with walls of brick or stone and roofs of slate or tile. The few remaining older houses were to be refronted to give a uniform appearance. The Market Hall was built in 1670 and it originally stood on open arches, the space beneath being used for stalls. It was enclosed in the nineteenth century and is now the county museum. When Celia arrived in Warwick there was much work still to be done, including the restoration of the church.

Celia then visited Stoneleigh which has changed a great deal since her time. It is now largely the Royal Agricultural Society's headquarters and the National Equestrian Centre. This is the nerve centre of equestrian activities in this country and Celia would no doubt have been fascinated to learn how the horse declined in this country with the advent of motor transport but then came back with the increase in leisure activities.

From Warwick she rode towards Daventry along part of the Vale of the Red Horse, which was a very heavy way. She probably rode on part of what is now the A425. We were grateful for a lift in the trailer and were then ready to tackle the next section which would, indeed, constitute the last lap of the Northern Journey. We unloaded with spirits high and I climbed aboard and set off towards our first bridleway, only to find that it was non-existent. If I had been riding using the 1:25 000 Ordnance Survey maps I might have been able to find trace of it but it is not practicable to attempt a ride such as I was doing and carry the necessary number of maps: as it was, I had already ''ridden across'' twenty five Ordnance Survey maps. Yet again I was being frustrated by the absence of bridleways which were clearly marked on the map; one which I tried was a towpath but it was impossible to reach it and, even if I had been able to, Cameron would have been too tall to go under the bridges. Perhaps it was as well that I could not get down to the bridleway because if I had reached the bridge and found passage impossible there was nowhere to turn a horse. Anyone who sets off to ride bridleways on the basis of what is marked on the Ordnance Survey map is in for some very unpleasant surprises. In the end there was nothing for it but to make my way round by road.

Celia crossed the Fosse Way and also the Welsh Road which can still be traced as a drover's route, indeed the name appears on road signs and one can even see places where the drovers rested and watered their animals. The Welsh Road is probably of older origin and was in existence long before it began to be used by drovers who were, of course, active in Celia's time.

The Vale of the Red Horse takes its name from a hill figure in the shape of a horse which was cut into the red soil near Sun Rising Hill. The figure was cleaned annually on Palm Sunday at the expense of a freeholder who held certain lands by dint of performing this service. The horse was destroyed at the time of the enclosures in 1798 but, because the associated fair was in danger of dying out, another horse was carved in an adjacent field. There had been suggestions that the original horse was caused by a freak of nature, lightning, planetary influence or whatever, akin to the description of fossils of living creatures as "sports of nature". The Rev Richard Jago dismissed the freak of nature theory and pointed out, sensibly, that the horse was more likely a symbol of Saxon conquest. The broad expanse of hill country stretching from Faringdon to Edgehill is certainly bounded by the Vale of the White Horse to the south and the Vale of the Red Horse to the north. The colours red and white do point to a possible mythological connection.

Nearby was Sunrising Inn which was a noted coaching inn, well known to travellers for its dinners and its port but now, sadly, a private residence with not even its original name as a reminder of its past history. Celia studied that area in some detail during her visits to Broughton Castle which was owned by her brother and is still in the family.

Like Celia I went to visit the site of the battle of Edgehill but found it to be in a valley with no public access. Her father and grandfather fought there, as did the grandfather of her host at Shuckburgh Sir Charles Shuckburgh. The grandfather, Sir Richard, found himself hunting between the two sides near Edgehill not knowing of the war. On learning of the conflict he immediately returned home, gathered together all his tenants and returned to join in the fray.

Celia's horses were very tired when she neared Shuckburgh and, seeing her distress, Sir Charles provided her with hospitality, including a good supper, wine and beds. She comments how Shuckburgh is on a high hill and certainly at the end of a long day it would be quite a climb to reach it. The house has a grey, cold and austere appearance and probably, except for the gardens, has altered little since her time. I hoped that my earlier problems were now over and that the way would be clear; I set off on a fresh, jumpy Cameron who was ready to spook at anything and began to ride through the park. At the first farm I enquired whether I was on the correct route, I was assured that I was and spent some minutes chatting to the farmer who much admired my horse. He insisted on opening and closing the first gate for me and pointed out that a few of the gates ahead would require me to dismount. As I rode across a field containing many beasts, a large bullock stood menacingly on a small eminence and it was with much trepidation that I rode past him. Cameron obviously appreciated the situation and crept past in an almost cat-like manner. Once past I realised that my throat had dried right up, obviously as a result of the fear which I had felt arising from my earlier encounters with bulls.

Across the park there was much evidence of ridge and furrow but, unusually, one could see them running in two directions at right angles, the result of the lie of the land and its division into furlong strips. In Celia's time the canal had not been built and with the perspective of history one can see that another cycle has occurred. The canals in this area were used for carrying coal, materials for the brewery at Oxford and for other commercial purposes. Now its commercial use has, sadly, declined but a new leisure use has grown up. It was delightful to see a gaily painted pleasure craft apparently making its way across the fields, the canal itself being quite invisible from my viewpoint. At nearby Southam there used to be overnight stabling for the barge horses and mules together with storage for bargees' provisions.

I continued in a south-easterly direction and for a short while encountered no difficulties and was able to enjoy the ride and the scenery. I missed out Daventry but returned there later without Cameron as I needed to make some purchases. I was fascinated to find a body of young people singing hymns and preaching the gospel in a shopping precinct. Celia would no doubt have been encouraged by this continuation of an old preaching tradition. The youngsters belonged to an organisation called ''Jesus soldiers'' which has been criticised by some because of the hold which is allegedly exerted on the followers, rather as with The Moonies. However, they were well presented in every way and their pleasant manner, happy faces and lively singing helped to brighten a somewhat dull and wet day.

From Upper and Lower Catesby, the sites of a former monastery and of deserted villages, I found myself on a gated road, one of a number in the area. The wind had been steadily increasing in strength during the day and was by this time up to gale force. I followed byways over open countryside and at the village of Charwelton saw the old packhorse bridge, of one horse width only and with low parapets to avoid damage to the packs. At this point the heavens opened and my concern became one of getting on rather than stopping to study history. Thence I continued south to Preston Capes, noting as I progressed a ridge along which can be traced an ancient road leading to Northampton. However, my way made use of quiet roads and byways. To begin with, the surface was excellent but just before I reached Canons Ashby the surface deteriorated and I encountered large ridges and undulations; this was to continue for the next mile or so and things were made even worse by the extremely wet conditions underfoot. Canons Ashby has been since the sixteenth century the home of the Dryden family; the house contains Elizabethan wall paintings and has a formal garden with terraces but Celia makes no mention of the house on this ride or on any previous ones, although her route must have taken her near it on several occasions. It is another of her somewhat surprising omissions.

The bad condition of the track became even worse and I had other problems to contend with. The gates were becoming increasingly difficult, only one could be opened from Cameron's back and another consisted of a gate frame propped up with two flimsy pieces of wood and with barbed wire and old gateposts trailing on the lane. Even tackling this one dismounted was a job in itself and in propping it back up I had the chagrin of seeing it collapse again twice before I could get the absurd structure to stay up. There was a flock of sheep grazing in the field and I was amazed that a farmer could risk his stock in this way. I had the feeling that he might well have been the sort of person who grumbles about people leaving gates open.

Eventually we reached Banbury Lane which is another road once used by drovers but of prehistoric origin, running for twenty two miles between Banbury and Northampton. Drovers from Wales would join it at the Rollright Stones and follow it northwards, the road meeting up with the Welsh Road at Culworth where there is a large market cross.

My original intention had been to miss out riding towards Northampton but with a large number of bridleways shown on the map I thought of riding at least to Courteenhall, which I had visited as a child, or to nearby Quinton. So I turned left onto Banbury Lane which was a delightful green lane to begin with. However, had I known what was in store I would have carried on southwards. For a longish stretch the undulations were so severe that it was like riding a switchback and poor Cameron had to struggle over all this mess, while I had to contend with low branches and ended up with a bruised back and scratches. I think that I really have to rate that as the worst bridleway which I have ever ridden! As we neared Adstone Lodge the surface did improve and I managed to negotiate the next bridleway although it was ploughed out. After that, however, I could not even find the start of the next bridleway or any trace of it along its supposed route. Reluctantly, I cut back up to Banbury Lane, at that stage a metalled road, and proceeded along it for the rest of the day.

When eventually I arrived at the night's stabling my hostess expressed no surprise at my account of the state of the bridleways, rather she was surprised that I should have expected anything else. I had noted many horses in the area and I wondered where they were ridden, presumably not on the bridleways.

Celia liked Northampton, describing it as "...a large town well built, the streetes as large as most in London except Holborn and the Strand, the houses well built of brick and stone some all stone, very regular buildings; the town hall is new built all stone and resembles Guildhall in little; tho' it is a good lofty spacious place there is two Barrs in it with the benches and seat distinct, over one of the Barrs is King William and Queen Mary's pictures at length".

Next day my way continued across forest areas to Whittlewood Forest which was one of the large royal hunting forests. There is evidence from extensive surveys of woodland carried out in Elizabethan times that these forests then thrived; for instance, the number of oaks in the crown forests of Northamptonshire increased from 85,000 in 1565 to 130,000 in 1608. After the heavy rain I much appreciated the change in the weather and I rode in warm sunshine, with Cameron in good form, working my way by bridleways across to Stony Stratford. The state of the bridleways had, mercifully, improved since the previous day and, except for one which I could not find a way along, they were all open although very wet underfoot and with heavy going. We were still in an undulating landscape with hedges and stock in fields and I was delighted that when I had to venture onto the metalled road the drivers whom I encountered were all exceptionally courteous. The average driver probably has little idea just how vulnerable a rider can feel on the road.

On then to Stony Stratford which is now bypassed and access to it restricted so that it retains its old charm, with interesting architecture and large inn signs projecting over the road. But the lace-makers noted by Celia have long since gone. They made pillow lace which was called bone lace, its name coming from the carved bone spindles or bobbins used in its manufacture. There is an excellent description of making bone lace in "Lark Rise to Candleford" in which Queenie was a constant attraction when she was making lace. The children around loved to see the bobbins being tossed hither and thither, seemingly at random, every bobbin being weighted with a bunch of bright beads. While this was going on, the lace makers would often be gathered around the fire, gossiping and singing as they worked. When each piece of lace was completed, it was wrapped in blue paper and a whole year's work sold annually at Banbury fair.

Many children were engaged in this activity, which helped to prevent their being a burden on the parish and limit the importation of Belgian lace from places such as Bruges. One can readily imagine people sitting on the doorsteps working at this activity as one can see lace makers in Bruges today.

I joined the newly created Swan's Way just south of Old Stratford, skirting the new city of Milton Keynes. The Swan's Way is the latest long distance bridleway created by the Countryside Commission with help from local riders. It runs from south of Northampton to Goring-on-Thames and provides bridleway riding for its whole length which includes some urban areas. It joins up with The Great Ridgeway and thus constitutes part of a larger network. I now found myself riding through flatter countryside but was surprised that I still had to open and close many gates although there was no stock in evidence. The first gate was impossible to open from Cameron's back and, even more irritatingly, it had been slammed in our faces when we were only three strides away. I had to dismount to open it and, after I had remounted, we squelched our way southward.

In a mile or so, I was delighted to find that an all weather riding surface had been put down and this made the going so much easier. The whole way to Little Horwood was helpfully waymarked by a horse shoe symbol with a swan inside it. At Great Horwood, another place where Celia stayed, I spent some time trying to locate the house where Celia stayed but without success. There were two possibilities: the old Manor, which has now been converted into flats, or Horwood House, which turned out to date from 1911 and to have been built on the site of an older house. I learnt this from the people at Horwood House, which is now owned by British Telecom, who were eager to help me in my enquiries. Time was pressing, however, and further enquiry at that stage was not possible as I had to continue my journey southwards.

18

Great Horwood to St Albans

As I prepared to set off on the last leg of my journey, with about only fifty more miles to go, it suddenly dawned on me that my goal of completing the Northern Journey was now within sight. My fears about undertaking the venture had been many but Cameron had proved perfectly able to undertake the mileages and stay in strange stables and I had been able to cope with his continuing unpredictability. The bridleways had varied very much from county to county and also within counties; if they had all been open the ride would have been even more pleasurable and, of course, much easier.

It was disappointing that there are very few bridleways between Great Horwood and Woburn and one has no alternative but to use metalled roads. The bridleways that there are, however, do have good surfaces, are open and take one through pleasant scenery. However, there was a compensation in using the roads in that I happened to catch sight of the church in Stewkley and it was so obviously Norman that I felt compelled to stop and go inside. I had chanced upon what is apparently one of the three remaining Norman churches in the country, with characteristic round arches and extensive dog-tooth decoration. It is this sort of happy discovery which provides an exciting fillip on cross-country rides. Stewkley will remain indelible in my memory as the village with the lovely Norman church.

Travelling on from Stewkley, I entered the wide main street of Woburn lined with impressive buildings. The Abbey is situated within a vast park with many fallow and, unusually, red deer. The park was smaller in Celia's time as in the eighteenth century there was much expansion and fields from the neighbouring parishes of Upper and Lower Gravenhurst and Husborne Crawley were taken in by emparkment. Husborne Crawley lost half its houses as well. The Russells, the family name of the owners of the house, did not live in the house continually until 1626, preferring their town house in London. They were driven out of London by the plague in common with many other families of the time.

Woburn Abbey is still owned by the the Dukes of Bedford as it was in Celia's time. It has been open to the public for many years with the father of the present Duke acting as a trailblazer in this respect. The house which Celia visited was still a Tudor building but the gardens were new. It was here that she made one of her few references to sports or games, commenting on the existence of a bowling green. The gardens were described as having topiary in the shape of several beasts and there were many arbours and seats; one ascended a flight of fifty steps to a vantage point from which deer hunting could be watched. The three large gardens were full of fruit, a large sweet gooseberry, orange and lemon trees, cherries and aloes. There was also a life-like stone effigy of a woman weeding which Celia took at first to be a real person. It was meant as a bird scarer and was apparently an effective one. Sadly all the formal gardens have gone, leaving only areas of grass and the steps.

Landscaping was carried out by Humphrey Repton a century after Celia's visit and it is likely that he carried out the changes which are apparent. Another change instituted this century was, of course, the famous safari park. I was fortunate to see bison as well as zebra and Przevalsky horses, including a foal, close to the perimeter fence. It is likely that Celia would have been flabbergasted to see these members of the horse family. The zebra is very closely related to the horse as we know it, indeed they have been successfully ridden and driven. The Przevalsky horse was known as an early equine but was believed to be extinct in the wild until 1966 when a Hungarian entomologist visited Western Mongolia and surprised the world, in Professor Challenger fashion, by reporting the existence of a herd there. They had withdrawn to an area seldom visited even by Mongolian nomads and were difficult to approach. Their name derives from a Russian explorer who first found them in the late 1800s and they represent a primitive form of horse which can, it is believed, be traced back to legends about Genghis Khan and to drawings of wild horses on vases and cave walls in Mongolia dating back to 2000 BC.

I walked through the public rooms of the house which contain many portraits of members of the family, including those who would probably have been there at the time of Celia Fiennes' visit. I was thrilled to see the de Caus grotto in the basement as this room is the oldest in the Abbey, and is vaulted with the ceiling decorated with Arabesques executed in shells. The walls are of simulated rock and coral formations, the frieze showing putti riding on dolphins and sea gods drawn on shell chariots: it has been rightly described as a startling revival of the magical world of the late Renaissance.

Celia then went to Dunstable via Hockliffe. She describes the road as sad, full of deep sloughs and impassable in winter. There was, however, a good pitched causey for foot travellers and horses which was raised above the road. She was talking about Watling Street, now the A5 trunk road. She visited Dunstable which in her time had a great water in the street like a large pond. The town was full of inns, in the eighteenth century there were over twenty in the four main streets and it was an important posting station for travellers en route to Chester and Holyhead from London. At high season as many as eighty coaches a day would pass through the town.

Dunstable is an ancient town, there was a pre-Roman settlement and it lies at the junction of Watling Street and the Icknield Way. It was also the site of one of the Eleanor crosses but this, together with the others which have now gone, was destroyed during the Civil War. I must confess that I was disappointed with present day Dunstable: most of the inns had gone and there was nothing of the atmosphere one associates with former staging towns. The High Street did nothing to excite my eye and I had no inclination to linger as I had in other places.

From Dunstable I took a northern route to the east of Luton and Hockliffe and joined what is hoped will become the Icknield Way long distance path for riders. Hockliffe is said to be the place which Bunyan had in mind when he wrote about the slough of despond in "Pilgrim's Progress". The road through there was known in the seventeenth century as one of the worst in the country: horses would frequently go down and their riders suffer injury. Because of these appalling conditions, Hockliffe was enclosed as early as 1620, the open fields being spoilt and trodden by cattle, sheep, park horses and hackneys. This heavy traffic had resulted from the nearness of Watling Street with the driving of cattle to and from Leighton Buzzard and other places. One has to remember that the upkeep of the roads then was the responsibility of the individual parishes and the parish of Hockliffe must have found it an impossible task to cope with the heavy traffic. In winter the road would be impassable and travellers would trespass on nearby land, the result being that the road would become as much as a hundred yards wide. This road was used by the Welsh cattle drovers and in 1669 the parish burial records show that a Welsh drover boy died travelling to Smithfield market.

It was appropriate that I passed through Hockliffe, the scene of the original slough of despond, in the three hundredth anniversary year of the death of Bunyan. He served for a short while as a Cromwellian soldier and it is likely that Celia would have heard of him, as an author if not as a soldier. She made no reference to him when she visited Bedford but references of that kind are rare in her journal. From Hockliffe we climbed onto the ridge northwards, passing under the M1 and following the bridleways towards Telegraph Hill, taking the opportunity on the good going to trot and canter steadily on.

Soon I crossed the Drays Ditches which are possibly of Iron Age or earlier origin. They lie over an enclosed ditched area which is thought was either a defensive work guarding a prehistoric trackway or was used as some form of cattle corral when free-ranging animals were rounded up. There is, however, no evidence of settlement in the area. Although we were close to the busy town of Luton there was some lovely scenery, but my enjoyment was marred by the number of motor cyclists on the track and adjacent land, using the area illegally for scrambling and off the road riding. I was very pleased that Cameron took this in his stride but I spent my time threatening the motor cyclists with my whip to persuade them to give me a wide berth. I felt that the many walkers, picnickers and parents with young children around must have shared my reaction to this intrusion. I even saw some motor cyclists riding their machines round picnic tables.

From Telegraph Hill my way dropped southwards across the busy A505 which follows the route of the Icknield Way. I left the main road to go into the village of Great Offley which is now bypassed but I was horrified to find that vehicles, including buses, were treating this byroad as if it were a motorway, rushing downhill at sixty or seventy miles an hour. To be on the safe side, I led Cameron up the steep hill into the village. I was soon safely on the bridleways which were very wet after even more heavy rain and I made my way southwards in warm sunshine.

The countryside was pretty and undulating with small hedged fields which betrayed evidence of a medieval farming pattern resulting from the acquisition of land by peasants. One particular family, the Deards, built up their holdings of land until, by the seventeenth century, they had become substantial yeoman farmers. This pattern recurs elsewhere in Hertfordshire which has fewer manors than neighbouring counties. As always, it was exciting to see historical evidence so clearly displayed as I rode. I did come across a little later what looked like the remains of the wooden pales of a ring park fence near King's Walden, which might possibly have been part of a fence which has been commented on by Oliver Rackham the countryside historian.

How delightful it was not only to observe the countryside but to ride through an area in which all the bridleways were open, signposted and waymarked, and with good albeit wet surfaces. Furthermore, all the drivers I met were most courteous in slowing down to prevent any possible alarm being caused to Cameron. There was, however, one nasty moment when, trotting uphill, we were met by a tractor driver cutting the hedge. He showed no sign of slowing down and seemed to be bent on colliding with us. I was unsure whether to turn tail or to turn wide into the field. I took the latter course and to my amazement the tractor continued past without easing. On occasions such as this I wonder, as a rider of many decades' experience, how an inexperienced rider would fare.

I continued on my way to Ayot St Lawrence along narrow lanes, through the same sort of intimate countryside which I had been riding through earlier. I passed Shaw's Corner, the house which was Bernard Shaw's home for over forty years. It is a former rectory which was built at the beginning of the century and has no architectural pretensions, but it is a homely place and has the feel of the great man from the moment one enters. Everything has been left as it was when he was there, even to a postcard in the kitchen stamped and ready to be posted. Not only is the house a monument to Shaw, it is also a reminder of what domestic life was like in the 1930s before television and other modern contrivances altered our way of life completely. He died in the 1950s but he was clearly not keen on keeping up to date. The kitchen, for instance, has an Eagle range which had to be blackleaded regularly and the bathroom was very old fashioned, although it has to be borne in mind that his London flat had no bathroom at all. The views from the house of the garden extending into the countryside beyond were quite lovely and one can see why he was attracted to the house and decided to buy it having leased it for some time.

I continued to my finishing point of St Albans, a place which Celia visited. It has been an important place since Roman times because of its situation at the junction of Watling and Akeman Streets and the Via Devana, which indeed I followed for a short distance and took note of the agger which was still visible. She liked the town, as it then was, with its Abbey, market place and wide main street with a church at each end. The Abbey was though, as she put it, much out of repair and mourned for someone to carry out necessary repairs. It is long since repaired, of course, and the city is thriving, although the Market Place has been largely rebuilt and the few houses dating back to 1640 have to be sought out. There is also an old bell tower which was once used to ring curfew, close to the site of an Eleanor cross which has now gone.

I had already decided, for reasons of practicality, to end my northern ride here. It was with a sense of achievement that I recalled that I had, with the exception of industrial areas and busy towns, ridden from Cheshunt in Hertfordshire to Scarborough in Yorkshire, back over Derbyshire and south to St Albans. The ride had enabled my horse Cameron to mature and he was very obviously a much bolder horse compared with when he started. I had, mercifully, completed the ride without being thrown off but I had suffered minor injury when we both fell in Elton Park. Also, Cameron had twice lost a front shoe but he had not suffered any lameness or a sore back, despite being bitten under the saddle by a horse fly on one occasion. One thing which struck me as curious was that I had met so few other riders or walkers on the complete journey. My feeling is that they keep to the well known paths or trails and do not explore on their own. Certainly had I not known that there are over three million horse riders in this country I would never have guessed it from my observations.

I felt something at one with the person who had inspired my journey, Celia Fiennes, in that my vision had been enlarged by it. I had learnt a great deal about my own country, indeed I had at least partially filled a gap in my knowledge which I had not realised existed.

17th C grain store

Part III

East Anglia, Part of the 1698 Journey

Ridden on Rowan in 1983

19

Ipswich to Norwich

Ipswich was described by Celia Fiennes in 1698 as ‘‘that very clean town’’. In 1982 it was, in the correspondence columns of the East Anglian Daily Times, called ‘‘the dirtiest town in England’’.

In the seventeenth century Ipswich was a busy port with shipbuilding also being carried on. There were probably more than a hundred ships based in Ipswich, a large number of which were colliers which transported coal from the north down to London.; when the seas were rough and London had sufficient for its winter needs these ships would be laid up in Ipswich. Other important cargoes were hay for the huge horse population of London and corn grown locally for London and also for The Netherlands. In addition to cargo there was a great deal of fishing so the Orwell must always have been alive with ships. It is still a busy port today, even though the shipbuilding and the fishing have gone. There are mills and other manufacturing facilities near the docks and large ships are always in and out of this busy port.

Ipswich at that time had a busy market covering a wide area and it was reckoned that upwards of six hundred people on horseback and foot would bring their wares into the town to sell. It was an altogether busy and lively town. The market ceased business only in recent times. The buttermarket is there in name but the butter is neatly wrapped and is certainly not sold out in the open by the pint.

Celia wrote "... so I went to Ipswitch, this is a very clean town and much bigger than Colchester is now, Ipswitch has 12 churches, their streetes of good size well pitch’d with small stones, a good Market Cross railed in, I was there on a Satturday which is their market day and saw they sold their butter by the pinte, twenty ounces for six pence ... Their Market Cross has a good carving, the figure of Justice carv’d and gilt." Unfortunately the market cross was swept away by the Victorians but there is still a good number of churches in the town centre, including many nonconformist churches dating back to Celia’s time. Defoe comments that there was a meeting house for the Presbyterians and one for Independents and the Quakers. The tradition of nonconformity in East Anglia remains as strong as ever. One needs to remember that when Celia saw Ipswich it had changed little since Saxon times and it was not until the Victorian era that the considerable expansion took place, bringing it to the same size as Norwich in terms of population.

Even today, the layout of the roads in the town centre is essentially medieval, highlighted by the fact that the road along the northern side is called Tower Ramparts. The Victorians did, however, sweep away much of historic value in addition to the market cross and changed the appearance of the town substantially. Around the turn of the seventeenth century Ipswich was known as an accessible place as one could readily get passage to London by coach or water. There were good houses available with low rents and a plentiful supply of provisions of all kinds, indeed it was said that a family could live here more cheaply than in any other town in the country.

Close to the town centre is the former home of the Earls of Hereford. Christchurch Manor, or Mansion as it is now known, is still intact but as a museum albeit a homely one which is devoted to everyday life. The history of the house is not clear; certainly it is very old and is said to date from a religious foundation, possibly a priory. The lovely park is still there, open to the public as it always was, but much altered are the gardens and gone are the large summerhouse, fine greenhouse, gravel walks and many fruit trees noted by Celia. Sadly the 1987 hurricane caused extensive damage to many of the old trees. It was here that the first Suffolk Shows were held before the present showground on the Felixstowe road was laid out. Shortly after Celia's time Defoe noted close by a physic garden belonging to a Dr Beeston; evidently he was a skilled botanist and had built up a collection of rare and exotic plants unrivalled in the country.

It was with a sense of anticipation that I saddled, bridled and mounted Rowan and headed north out of Ipswich, preparatory to swinging north east and making for Woodbridge. Rowan was striding out at his customary fast walk and we went not by the deep lanes which Celia used but by bridleways in order to avoid the busy

A12. These bridleways were all open, with good surfaces and many through lanes with hedges on both sides which all made for very pleasant riding through undulating, mainly arable landscape. After ten easy miles and then crossing the busy A12 without difficulty we arrived at Woodbridge.

The medieval town plan is still evident, despite the inevitable changes which have occurred. The old narrow streets and alleyways are still there, as is the market place where there is a small but lively market every Thursday. Celia also comments that Woodbridge had great meetings for dissenters: the Quaker Meeting House was built in 1678 at a time of religious intolerance, and within months of its construction and first use the local justices declared that the meetings of ''five persons or more of the age of sixteen years and upwards'' were illegal and ordered the Friends or Quakers ''peaceably to disperse...to their several homes and abodes and not break His Majesty's peace by meeting in such an unlawful manner''. The persecution even led to a Quaker martyr who died in nearby Melton gaol in 1684 as a direct result of his imprisonment for his beliefs.

Schooners were built in Woodbridge to take produce, hay and straw to London for the large horse population and the dairy cows that were kept close to London. In summer you can cross the river by ferry which is an ideal route for visitors to the Sutton Hoo burial site. The Deben mud, well known to all local sailors, would inhibit any attempt to ford the river now but until recent times there was a causeway which could be used for this purpose at low tide. The hulks of the old iron barges can still be seen but almost all the river traffic now is pleasure craft, for which the river provides a challenge to sailors as well as scenery of great beauty, not for nothing is one part of the river named Troublesome Reach.

We rejoined the bridleway on the north bank of the Deben and rode on delightful sandy tracks with views down the river and with many sailing craft to be seen; then we headed inland across Sutton Heath and into Rendlesham Forest with the almost continuous noise of aircraft from the American base. If Rowan could see the planes he simply cocked his head and looked at them but if they came up from behind they terrified him. We would then usually end up in an uncontrollable gallop with saddlebags flapping madly in every direction. He takes a lot of pulling up but eventually he settled back into his

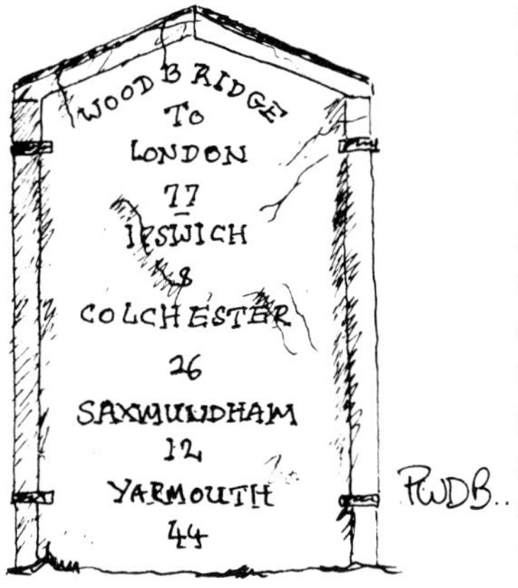

easy gait and we continued on our way to Butley Priory, a former religious foundation dating from 1171.

We proceeded by means of the tracks in Tunstall Forest and across the Common, heather lined with springy going and with silver birch and conifers around. These tracks form a maze which is not easy to follow because they are not clearly defined and tend to be signed, quite wrongly, as footpaths. Skirting the edge of sugar beet fields, a crop unknown in seventeenth century England, we arrived at Snape maltings. Industrial and social change has altered the maltings into the famous concert hall, the inspiration of Benjamin Britten and Peter Pears. Sadly, neither is now with us but their memory is indelible. One is reminded of the instruction to those who seek a memorial to Christopher Wren in St Paul's Cathedral to ''look about you''.

The buildings overlook the marshes and the River Alde, on which a sailing barge had her dark red sails hoisted in readiness for a pleasure trip. I tried to take a photograph from the saddle but the sails suddenly flapped in the wind, Rowan jiggled and jumped and I had to concentrate on steadying him as, to make things even more difficult, cars sped by. Having managed to settle him, I turned my gaze to the roadside fields where a second crop of hay was being gathered on the low-lying meadows close by.

Up a nearby lane on what I expected to be a bridleway I was greeted by a notice which proclaimed ''footpath - no vehicles'', so I went the long way round along the main Aldeburgh road. Then, maddeningly, at the other end of the track was a bridleway sign. Would Celia Fiennes have begun to understand our modern frustrations?

Just as she had three centuries before, I rode in sight of the sea, along the dunes from Sizewell to Minsmere and on to Dunwich. She probably rode either on the road that is now the A12 or along the ancient trackways that radiate from Dunwich. In her time this sparsely populated area would have been fraught with danger from highway robbers or other hazards. The heath which she crossed has been like this since Bronze Age times but going further back it was likely to have been forest. The sea that day was, for the east coast, unusually blue with small white horses and on the marshes and water meadows cattle were quietly grazing. This was ideal riding, trotting and cantering along the coastal tracks beside which harebells (the true bluebells of Scotland) waved in the wind.

Dunwich in the middle ages was a busy thriving port but several disastrous storms over two centuries caused the cliffs to fall away and a mass of shingle to bury the old town, block the river and destroy the harbour. Defoe commented that the town seemed in danger of being swallowed up and, indeed, several years after his visit there was yet another disastrous storm. In his time there was still a great deal of shipping carrying butter, cheese and corn but all that remains now are a few fishing boats which are launched from the beach and a tiny town, no larger in size than a small village.

From Dunwich I had superb views of the sea as I started off along forest tracks and quiet roads towards Blythburgh, not Blyford as stated in the 1982 edition of Celia Fiennes. Blythburgh has a magnificent church looking out over the marshes which were created by defensive flooding during the Second World War. I stopped for lunch at at the old coaching inn "The White Hart". After the morning's ride I was ready to enjoy the excellent trout with salad washed down with lager, sitting in the garden holding Rowan in one hand and feeling a sea breeze blowing and watching a slight mist moving inland. What is now the garden and car park of the inn was, in Celia's time, part of the quay which trading vessels used regularly. In earlier times still Blythburgh was a busy market town and had its own court. All that is left is a handful of houses.

Blythburgh Church is known as the church of the marshes and is my favourite Suffolk church. It has hardly altered over the centuries; the hoof-prints of Cromwell's horses can still be seen at the rear and arrowheads have been found embedded in the angels up in the roof from the time of desecration. One wonders how Celia viewed the actions of Cromwell's men as she was the daughter of one of his colonels. Rings for tying up cattle or horses are still to be seen at the back of the church and at one time the building was also used as a barn. Nearby, in the garden of a house called The Priory, are the remains of an Augustinian priory founded as a cell of St Osyth around 1120.

It was probably a long while since a horse had been ridden out from the inn. Rowan hesitated slightly at the double white lines on the busy A12 and we clambered onto the narrow grass verge with cars speeding by, allowing no room for a side-step or other error. Celia would have crossed the river here by a wooden bridge and recently traces of an old bridge across the Blyth have been found which is likely to have been the very bridge she used.

From here I rode to Blyford, the next village, where a peaceful scene greeted me of people drinking in the garden of the pub opposite the small church. The road runs high above the low-lying meadows along what Celia would have called a "causey", the same as our word "causeway". These low-lying meadows were flooded deliberately in the winter as a method of fertilisation, then drained so that a hay crop could be taken. We skirted Holton and went on to Westhall. The way was signposted as a footpath and led on to a Second World War airfield, now the home of Le Grys Turkeys. We plodded along the old runways, with the smell of turkeys very evident in the air; what a desolate spot and, to make things worse, the bridleway had disappeared and there seemed no way out. After trying several dead ends, climbing over fallen trees and pushing through brambles I found a helpful turkey worker, one man to look after over twenty turkey houses apparently, who gave me directions back to the road.

At Westhall I joined another rider who was exercising under saddle her father's chesnut driving cob; we rode together for a short while and talked about the disappearance of the bridleway. We passed by the hunt kennels which are in complete isolation and it crossed my mind that saboteurs could easily wreak havoc there. I believe the kennels belong to the Waveney Harriers who, as their name indicates, hunt the hare on horseback, there being no fox hunting in this part of the country. Rowan had heard the hounds, of course, and his head came up and he started jiggling about, probably with thoughts of hunting which he loved.

My companion of the previous few miles could tell me nothing of the way ahead as we parted company. The next bridleway lay across Redisham Park, with open stubble fields and the line completely undefined. Careful map reading was necessary to enable us to head in the right direction and we crossed over a couple of bridges into the park itself. It was a beautiful route across parkland but difficult to find. The gates were well maintained but, even so, I had to dismount at each one to undo the chains.

As I neared the hall, I could see a herd of Friesian heifers running with a bull in the adjacent field. Suddenly, to my horror, the bull separated from the herd and charged angrily to the gate close by me, snorting and pawing the ground. I had never encountered anything like it in my life and hope never to do so again. ''Will the gate hold?'' was the thought in my mind. I quickly worked out that the only way of escape was to jump in and out of the nearby concrete yard. I would have had to clear two large five bar gates. They were within Rowan's capability as he was a superb and safe jumper but I certainly did not want to have to tackle such a series of obstacles under such extreme circumstances. Fortunately, however, the gate held and his jumping ability did not have to be put to the test. With the tension off, the idiotic thought entered my mind of the sign which was allegedly erected somewhere saying ''Entrance to this field is free - the bull will charge you later''.

We continued past the hall and our way took us into the next field where there were cattle grazing in the distance. I opened the gate and went through a little apprehensively in the light of my recent alarming experience. We walked quietly along the bank of a stream; halfway across the field the cattle saw us and three or four left the herd and headed in our direction. My heart was in my mouth but I continued at a steady pace, keeping an eye on their progress and wondering about another escape route. Fortunately they lost interest and put down their heads to continue grazing and for the second time within a few minutes I breathed a heartfelt sigh of relief. We reached the far side safely only to find at the edge of the park that we had to contend with a narrow bridge only two planks wide. Could Rowan manage it? He said no, so I dismounted and removed his saddle but there was still not enough width for a well endowed Cob. Turning back was out of the question so I saddled up again, clambered down with him to the stream, clearing undergrowth from the bank on the way, remounted and rode him across the river bed. I was really beginning to understand the sort of difficulties which Celia would have had to face as a routine matter and the sense of recreating the past had become very real to me. After all this excitement I rode quietly on to the village of Ringsfield on the outskirts of Beccles where I finished the day's ride, thankful that neither of us had come to any harm.

In 1697 Beccles was the third largest town in Suffolk. Today it probably ranks fourth after Ipswich, Lowestoft and Bury. It stands on a spur of high land which, since 1086, has been gradually reclaimed from the sea. At that time there was a thriving herring market and later a corn market was set up. The town has since become known for the printers William Clowes one of whose main tasks has been the printing of the Bible in many languages, of which Celia would no doubt have approved. Most villages around still have a chapel building, although some have been turned into private dwellings and Beccles boasted a large meeting house in which as many as four hundred people could listen to the minister.

Celia stayed at nearby Roos Hall when she passed this way. It had then been completed only within the previous hundred years, the builder being Thomas Colby, although there must have been a previous house as there is evidence of a medieval park and moat. The house is an unspoilt Tudor hall which has virtually no outbuildings and stands attractively close to the River Waveney. Celia's host was the then owner, Sir Robert Rich, who was a great supporter of the nonconformist meeting place in Beccles. She was there on a Sunday and we presume that they would have gone to worship together.

Beccles would still be recognisable by Celia. The fine church with its detached campanile, which houses a peal of ten bells, is still there, as is the market cross. She described the place as a sad Jacobitish town which chose no parliament men. It had, she averred, no good buildings. This reads oddly to us as she apparently had no regard for the timber framed buildings which we set great store by today.

The wooden bridge that Celia took over the River Waveney has long since gone. It was apparently a substantial structure with rails ; many bridges of the time would have been plank structures without the security of rails and anyone who has ridden a horse will realise how dangerous this would have been. The land around here is low and flat and when Celia rode this route the road lay under water; this was unsafe for strangers in particular because of the uncertainty of the surface with holes, quicksands and loose bottom. She comments again how long the miles in East Anglia were owing to the heavy going and how much easier it was to ride in Yorkshire.

From here the way to Norwich was mainly by metalled roads interspersed with a few bridleways and large greens which made for pleasant riding. I rode up to within a few miles of Norwich but not right into the city: I decided that it was safer to visit it without Rowan.

20

Norwich to Cambridge

Celia's description of her first sight of Norwich has a modern, and indeed a moving, ring for anyone who knows that city and appreciates its many attributes. "Norwitch opens to view a mile distance by the help of a hill whereon is a little village; as I observe most of the great towns and citties have about them little villages as attendants or appendix's to them which are sort of subburbs, there being stragling houses for the most part all the way between that and the gates; you pass over a high bridge that leads on over a high Causey of a pretty length which looks somewhat dangerous, being fenced with trenches from its bancks pretty deep to secure it from the water, and these trenches runns in many places round the low grounds to drain them, which are employ'd to whiten and bleach their woollen stuff the manufacture of the place; this long Causey brings you to a large stone bridge over the river into which those trenches empty themselves."

In her time the city was completely walled and full of towers and she noted the wide well pitched streets which were very clean. As she entered the city centre there was a large well house with a wheel to wind up the water for public use. A little farther on there was a large pond which was walled round: this again was water for public use. But, even more interestingly, not far from The Haymarket there was a water house and this supplied the city with piped water. All in all, Norwich was a special kind of place, presenting a pleasing aspect and well looked after and provided for. She noted that "On the Castle hill you see the whole City at once, being built round it, its a vast place and takes up a large tract of ground its 6 miles in compass.....the whole Citty lookes like what it is, a rich thriveing industrious place." The compactness of the city centre with much of the wall still in place helps impart a sense of homeliness. Indeed as recently as the time of Parson Woodforde, the diarist, the city gates were closed each night. It is also, as Pevsner reminds us, a city which has everything, with a cathedral (now two cathedrals), a major castle on a mound, an undisturbed medieval centre, thirty two medieval churches and a river.

The "blackish or shineing" flints used for facing are still very much in evidence. Norwich today has a thriving market place where fruit, vegetables, clothing, gifts and so on can be bought on any weekday. The cattle market and the annual horse fair on Maundy Thursday have been displaced from their traditional place in the city centre to the edge of the city, but in Celia's time there were many markets, reflecting the size of the city. Three times a year there were large cattle markets, for which beasts, about forty thousand a year is an estimate, were driven down from Scotland for fattening on the Norfolk marshes. These not only kept Norfolk supplied with beef but weekly consignments were driven to London as well. Norwich also had large hog and fish markets. Materials of all types, including the local worsted, calico and damask, could also be purchased. Norwich at this time was famous for its weaving and most of the population was employed with spinning and weaving. This manufacture was carried on in garrets on people's own looms or in combing shops; the place was said to be deserted on non-market days as everyone was busy indoors and emerged on market days and Sundays only.

The Town Hall ''esteemed the best'' has gone but the City Hall in its striking position at the top end of the covered market is held in high regard and is featured in many books on modern architecture, despite what Pevsner calls ''its frankly admitted dependence on Sweden''.

Norwich was one of the major towns, it was second in the country in the Middle Ages, which underwent structural change as a result of the Reformation. There were then as many as sixty churches; six had disappeared after the Black Death and seventeen were secularised during the middle years of the sixteenth century. That process has continued in our time and more churches have, sensibly, been found a new use as museums and so on. What has changed is the size of Norwich in relation to the other cities in the country. Celia noted that it had been displaced to third place by Bristol; by the time of the 1961 census it had become thirty-third.

What may seem odd to us is the way that she ignores the Anglican cathedral but comments on the number of dissenters in the city. Her view of things was undoubtedly affected by her background and belief: perhaps the way in which we look at ecclesiastical buildings in this age in terms of their architectural merit is a reflection of the changed attitude to religion.

I retraced my steps to just south of Norwich, collected Rowan, mounted and set off once more. There was supposed to be a bridleway leading off from the A140 Ipswich road but I could see no sign of it. Getting off the road was a matter of urgency as even on Rowan the fast moving lorries and other traffic were quite terrifying, so I escaped onto the first minor road. I went through the village of Wacton and past yet another hunt kennels, this time the Dunston. Our next bridleway, a wide green lane, looked inviting. I asked an elderly man cutting the hedge if the way was clear. He thought so and we set off at a brisk trot, only to find that the track soon vanished. I thought that I was on the wrong side of a hedge so we retraced our steps but then found a large stream which was not bridged. We half scrambled and jumped across and so got back onto the original track over the railway line. I really did hope that my difficulties were over for the present but within a few yards I was greeted by barbed wire barricading my way. I found a place to undo it and re-tied it behind me and then eventually, after coping with various lesser hazards, reached a metalled lane.

We took the low road to Bunwell beside water meadows and small cropped fields and over dry unbridged fords. I looked at the rushes in the stream and then spotted a round thatched stack, an unusual sight indeed. I dismounted and led Rowan for a mile or so to rest his back and allow me to stretch my legs. While walking I met an old man who asked me why I was leading; I explained and we continued chatting for about a quarter of an hour. It turned out that, in his youth, he used to help his father who worked as a groom. He wanted to know how far I had ridden, how much Rowan ate and how much a set of shoes cost. He told me what crops had been planted in the nearby fields and how, the previous year, the TV people had been down to film the local thatcher and the same sort of round stacks which I had just noticed. Before I took my leave he told me how, the previous year, some holidaymakers with a gypsy caravan and an undersized pony were using the whip excessively. He had chased after them, told them to get down and lead the pony, seized their whip and flung it into a field. They did not dare to retrieve it and it remained there still.

As I took my leave I reflected that one meets fewer people of the sort I had just been talking to. The old countryman or woman would stand at the gate and be ready to engage any passerby in conversation. Today people seem not to stand around idly and tend to use a car rather than travel on foot or by bicycle. Passing the time of day was once an established feature of country life and it seems to be one of those things which disappear without one noticing.

I remounted and rode onto the B1113 road. What a nightmare, the road was so slippery that Rowan's feet were slipping and sliding all over the place but we did manage to reach New Buckenham without mishap. This attractive small town with its market place and castle demanded time to explore. It was planned in pre-medieval times but did not expand as anticipated and remains the size of a large village. After a lager and a couple of rolls I photographed the market place, whipping post, nonconformist chapel and castle, then I remounted and carried on towards the sister town of Old Buckenham. My next bridleway was marked as a footpath and it went through an impressive looking stud. I had to carry on over the newly mown grass which might well intimidate some riders from using this perfectly legal right of way. Having reached the end of the bridleway I was in Old Buckenham with its enormous green, so large that it dwarfs the houses around its edge. Some fifty acres in extent, it is one of the largest in the country. Rowan began to pull at the grass while I spent a few moments in contemplation; his motto could well have been ''never waste time''.

After a night's rest we headed refreshed towards Thetford Forest, passing through Banham which boasts a zoo and a motor museum. The bridleway to Kenninghall, typical of the area, began as a wide metalled track and then continued as a green lane with hedges on either side. Autumn fruits in abundance, rosehips, hawthorn berries, elderberries and sloes, filled the hedges and it looked like being a good year for sloe gin. The track became narrower and brambles and brushwood impeded our progress, but Rowan pushed and clambered his way through to the village. There were horses grazing in fields at both ends of the bridleway so it seemed strange that there was no evidence of it being ridden. Where, I wondered for the umpteenth time, do these people ride?

Church Lane in Kenninghall has a row of unspoilt old houses and cottages, some of which, thank goodness, have not been modernised. Some even look as if they have come out of the pages of Edwin Cook and Olive Smith's book of cottages and farmhouses. I noted with pleasure such names as ''The Old Pumphouse'', ''Farrier's House'' and so on. The chapel is unusual in that it has gravestones at the front. The village looks full of history and, indeed, Mary Tudor stayed here in 1553 as a guest of the Duke of Norfolk at the time of the death of her brother, whence she rode post haste to Framlingham to be proclaimed queen.

I rode on towards East Harling and skirted Thetford Forest. This is not a forest which Celia would have seen but a twentieth century creation. It was planted in the Breckland, a vast sandy wilderness in which little could grow, to provide a source of home grown timber.

We crossed back into Suffolk over the old pack bridge at Knettishall Heath, the route which Celia might have taken, and across the old heath to the Rushford Belts (of trees). The route took us along a road with wide grass verges and Rowan broke into a canter for half a mile or so as it was so inviting. Large numbers of pigs were out in the fields, white pigs, brown pigs and slightly spotted ones. Whether they were self coloured or simply pigs which had gone dirty I could not be sure. In a short space of time I was in the tiny village of Euston where a thatcher was busy reroofing a cottage and where flowers were for sale at a cottage gate and I rode through the entrance of Euston Park.

Celia stayed here on her travels as a guest of the Duke of Grafton, whose family still owns it. I dismounted and went inside to look around. The famous Stubbs painting ''Mares and Foals'' caught my eye and I was thrilled to realise that it was painted just outside where I was standing but, of course, after Celia's time. The hall, standing in a large park with a perimeter of six miles, was built of brick with four towers surmounted by balls, the windows set low and the rooms of good size and height, with a long picture gallery. Since Celia's visit, however, the house was remodelled in about 1750 only to be completely destroyed by fire in 1900. The present coach house and stable block was built in 1755 and the gardens are simpler than they were, with trees now hiding the view of the church from the house. Originally the gardens were laid out with fountains and stone statues, a canal and walled courts. From the gardens several rows of trees ran the length of the park, opening up vistas from the front of the house. The gardens were altered to Kent's design in the century following Celia's visit in favour of the more open and natural style then preferred. Kent designed a folly in the form of a Palladian temple from which the Third and Fourth Dukes used to watch their racehorses being exercised in the park. Apart from Kent two other famous garden designers had a hand in altering the park, Evelyn and Capability Brown. Celia described the scenery around Euston as very like Salisbury Plain with ''the great winds'' blowing. This is no longer true today, the area has been afforested and farmed and is no longer an open plain.

Celia frequently took diversions during the course of her journeyings, and I decided to do the same. Instead of riding straight to Bury St Edmunds I set out to explore the bridleways marked on the Ordnance Survey map. There had been a change in the weather: it had become cloudy and damp, following a lovely spell of sunshine, with outbursts of heavy rain. My exploration began on the Elveden Estate on the old highway known as Shaker's Road. It is a broad, grassy road, possibly Roman, the name perhaps deriving from ''sheep's road''. There are various drover's routes in this area so such a derivation is quite likely. A few tractors were working the fields, but otherwise we were quite alone.

Suddenly Rowan stopped in his tracks with his head held high. Deer leaped across his path: they had strayed from the nearby forest. The track crossed an area of heathland and there was little guidance which way to take. However I managed to find the correct way really by following my nose. It had become quiet again following the irruption of the deer and the only background noise was the low sound of aircraft from the nearby American base at Lakenheath. They interrupted my musings about the Romans and jolted me back into the twentieth century. At the end of the road I dismounted to give Rowan a break and have some lunch. He made the most of the opportunity by grazing and browsing to replenish the energy he had expended during the morning.

I remounted and rode into Brandon, a small town which to me has a depressing air. I had hoped to ride on the towpath alongside the River Thet but all my attempts were frustrated by the absence of any defined path and eventually I gave up and rode back into the town. We went over the level crossing and entered the forest at the Harling Drove. The Drove, or Great Fen Road, connects the Fens with the southern end of Peddars Way, an ancient road from Colchester to North Norfolk. The Drove is probably Neolithic in origin, later Romanised and then in more recent times used by drovers to take animals and geese from the Fens into Norfolk. It is said that the Drove is the oldest road in the country.

In about a mile we turned into the forest; the heavens opened and we stood under the trees in an attempt to seek shelter but it was pointless and I decided to continue. Just north of here lies Grimes Graves or Devil's Graves as the place used to be called. The site is a group of neolithic flint mines. Some of the flints were fashioned into tools and there is evidence that some were taken to Avebury, the ancient site of religious observance in Wiltshire, by means of the Icknield Way.

We arrived at Santon Downham and carried on towards East Harling, our circular tour completed. Rowan was boxed back to Euston, ready for the next day's leg. It was said of Euston and the nearby villages in 1667 by John Evelyn, the famous forestry pioneer "The Travelling Sands about ten miles wide of Euston that have so damaged the country, routing from place to place like the sands of the desert of Libya, and have quite overwhelmed some gentlemen's whole estates". These sands have been stabilised by the planting of the forest and the scene has changed from the unremitting bleakness which Celia commented upon.

Celia no doubt rode straight into Bury but I decided to visit the town on foot. It was market day in Bury St Edmunds, or St Edmundsbury to give it its alternative title, and the cattle and street markets were in full swing. The car parks were full and people were crowding in on buses from various villages around. The scale of activity was no doubt greater than when Celia was here but in other respects there has probably been little change. The corn market dates from the last century but the basic road plan originated between 1066 and 1086. The two main streets are criss-crossed by four or five other streets, the town itself being situated on a hill with low lying meadows around.

The open space in front of the great abbey was for centuries the site of the great medieval fair. The ruins of the abbey are now surrounded by attractive gardens, a refuge from the hustle and bustle outside. Celia would have seen the two parish churches of St Mary's and St James' although they are no doubt in a better state of repair now. There were originally two other places of worship, the Quakers and the Anabaptists, but the original buildings have long since gone.

The Cupola House, where she stayed and which she describes at length, still stands out above the other houses although it is not now owned by an apothecary but is a wine merchant's and a coffee house. The sixty steps up from the road, by the way, give an indication of the change of street level over the centuries. This house had four rooms on each floor and they were all sizeable and high. There was a drawing room, a chamber full of china and a room with an embroidered damask bed. The two other rooms had mohair beds and below the parlours was a large shop. The item that excited Celia most was a herbal, in it was every sort of tree and herb cut and dried and pasted onto the pages of a book. It was owned originally by a doctor who left it as a legacy to the apothecary. Celia comments that she would like to have spent many days studying it but was only passing through Bury. She also makes reference to the old timber framed houses which are still much in evidence today and to the absence of any manufacturing in the town. This is still true today, the huge sugar beet factory and the industrial estates lying well away from the town proper.

The next day, hoping for better weather, I saddled up again and set off from Euston, riding through Barnham and down the Icknield Way through the King's Forest. Even in the rain and mist which had returned, this stretch never ceases to thrill me. The broad way is indescribably lovely, with a wide grassy expanse at each side of the track, and with the forest's silver birches, beeches, oaks, Corsican pines and Douglas firs beyond. At the foot of the trees, the harebells were drooping in the rain and the viper's bugloss was past its best. Time appears to stand still here as the Icknield Way has been a route since around 2500BC and many thousands of travellers must have ridden or tramped this way from North Norfolk to Avebury.

I rode towards Lackford past the Suffolk County Council picnic area. There were not many people around although even in those bad conditions there were several cars parked. Suddenly two riders appeared and, to my horror, began to jump the barriers and canter round the picnic tables. No wonder, I mused, that some people do not like horses! We who love horses must put ourselves in the place of those people who have no particular regard for them or may indeed be terrified of the creatures.

We continued on our way over the River Lark, one of Bury's two rivers, and into Lackford, a village on the Icknield Way. Six hundred urns were once found here which suggests that the villagers were cremated until their conversion to Christianity in the seventh century. In a short while we passed over an early medieval bridge and I dismounted and climbed down to examine it. It has been partially reconstructed but full marks, I thought, to the Suffolk County Council for leaving the original arches. The rain was still tipping down and I heaved myself aboard again with my wet clothes dragging me down. Map reading had become very difficult: my spectacles had become spotted with rain, my maps soaked and, to make matters even worse, Rowan was walking slightly sideways, ducking his head against the rain. Shortly I ceased to worry and as I rose to the trot I squelched; everything was soaked, all my clothes, Rowan and my tack. What an uncomfortable day it had been.

Moyse's Hall, Bury St Edmunds

We passed Cavenham Park and village and the road was lined with splendid beech trees. I was not, however, in a mood fully to appreciate the beauty around me and as we plodded on I was brought back into the twentieth century with a jolt, first by the sound of a train and then by the rumble of traffic on the busy A45 trunk road from the east coast to the midlands. The weather had become impossible, in places the roads were under water and car drivers were having to take care, but Rowan splashed through everything and I was reminded that water is an impediment to twentieth century traffic in the way that it was not in the seventeenth. We left the road and took a bridleway to Herringswell, along the way encountering a four wheel drive rally taking place in a quarry. The drivers were obviously thoroughly enjoying themselves, unlike their cousins on the roads. Mud was flying everywhere as the vehicles swooped up and down the steep slopes and I would have loved to stay and watch but I just had to finish the day's ride. We continued at a smart trot but Rowan suddenly stopped in a deep puddle, pawed the ground and made it clear that he wanted to roll. It took all my strength to prevent him going down, he was such a strong animal. I felt sure that he considered the whole episode a joke.

Then round the corner came four ''Thelwell'' ponies into view with small children on leading reins, probably from a local riding school. The conditions were certainly make or break for these youngsters learning to ride and I wondered whether any of them might find themselves involved in the same sort of activity as I in the years to come.

I passed Herringwell and continued, still on bridleways, to Chippenham. The landscape changed and thoroughbreds graced the well fenced paddocks, showing polite interest in us as we went by. I was loth even to turn my head though for fear that the movement would send more water down my neck. However, we were definitely making progress and were virtually within a stone's throw of Newmarket.

Out of the mist, the village of Chippenham and the Hall and Park appeared. What a clean and prosperous looking place it was. The whole village was created by the estate and Celia was very much taken with it, including the delightful gardens, well kept with gravel and green walks and walled in flower gardens. She admired the house also, with its fine silver and china and with its damask and velvet hangings. There were also beautiful wood carvings of beasts and fowls, fruit and herbage.

I reflected that one compensation for the miserable conditions was the fact that the bridleways had all been open, clear and easy to find. My main concern however was to dry out, having finished the day's ride, and settle Rowan for the night. Then I had to decide whether to visit Ely next. Cambridge was another possibility but the best bridleways run south, which would have meant another day's ride to get north again, heading towards either Huntingdon or Ely. As this was a ride of the twentieth century rather than a slavish recreation of the seventeenth century one, Cambridge won. It would also give me an opportunity to visit some of the interesting National Trust properties such as Wicken Fen, Wimpole Hall and Anglesey Abbey. I could select a route on or near the great defence ditches Devil's Dyke and Brent Ditch, or I could ride on the bridleways of Mare's Way and Street Way. All these names have a story to tell.

The next day we left Chippenham on a damp and misty morning, passing through the villages of Snailwell and Exning, where the market used to be before the "new market" was set up at the time of the Black Death, skirting Newmarket by means of metalled roads. The scenery at Exning was different from in Celia's time as it was enclosed in the late eighteenth century, mainly for the protection of the racehorses. There is a bridleway which bypasses the main A45 but my concern was whether it would be open all the way.

My concern, however, proved to be groundless. I found that the bridleway runs beside the A45, separated from it by a hedge for much of the way but near enough for us to be drenched with spray from passing lorries. In the adjacent fields sugar beet was being lifted and ploughing was going on. There was a cheery wave from each of the tractor drivers as they passed, how being on horseback encourages social contact of this sort.

By riding across Newmarket Heath from east to west one realises something of the size of the bloodstock industry. Studs abound, each one no doubt hopeful of rearing a future classic winner, and the town itself is full of training establishments. Even traffic lights can be operated by riders to give the horse priority and the railway station was clearly designed to facilitate the movement of horses. Racing at Newmarket was the sport of kings way back in Celia's time and horses would then have been raced in daily heats across the heath. Sadly so many of these horses were pushed to the limit that a few often died in the stables after the heats and later the system of holding heats before a race was given up.

Newmarket at this time was full of coffee houses and gaming tables where gentlemen would retire after the racing but Defoe comments that one would see no ladies there except for a few from gentlemen's families who would travel by coach to see a race and then return straight home. In those days there was very little formality to the racing and the races took place on the open heath, with spectators making their way there by coach or horseback. Three hundred years on, it is pleasant to record that the heath is still open to horse riders, walkers, fliers of model aircraft and the like.

Soon after Newmarket we crossed Devil's Ditch. It never ceases to amaze me that such an artefact can survive intact since the time of the Iceni in a highly industrialised country such as ours. We negotiated a short stretch of road and then came to a bridleway signposed "Byway to Great Wilbraham". The route should have been straightforward but the line of the Roman road had been lost at the point where one crosses the new A11 by a bridleway bridge. I missed the turning completely, something I had never done before, and finished up in the village of Bottisham where I had no intention of going. We were, however, close to Anglesey Abbey and to Wicken Fen, which was no bad thing and so I took the opportunity to visit them.

Anglesey Abbey is one of my favourite National Trust houses. The original priory was founded by Henry I in 1135 and it was probably a religious house for four centuries; the Augustinian canons assumed a black habit and hood and were known as the Black Canons. After the dissolution in 1535 the abbey passed to secular owners and in the early part of the seventeenth century Thomas Hobson, of "Hobson's Choice" fame, acquired what was left of the abbey. Hobson was, of course, the Cambridge carrier who refused to let any horse out for hire except in strict rotation.

In the house I particularly enjoy the dining room, based on the thirteenth century refectory, and the living room which was originally the chapter house. The gardens are a successful combination of formal gardens and landscape and are probably the finest gardens created in this country this century. Important royal events of this century have left their mark at Anglesey. In commemoration of Queen Elizabeth's coronation a garden was created by erecting on one of the lawns a large number of columns each weighing two tons, surrounding a statue of David. The Queen's silver jubilee prompted the replanting of trees bordering the daffodil walk and the coronation of King George VI and Queen Elizabeth was commemorated by an avenue 1400 feet long.

The gardens include the monks' garden which is an area of rough grass and old fruit trees in which four thousand bulbs have been planted. Other lawns have a variety of urns, vases and statuary in various materials including metal, marble, stone and composition. The subjects vary from a huntsman with his hounds to wrestlers and a series of busts of twelve Chinese emperors. There are many other avenues, rides, herbaceous borders and a quarry pool based on a place where coprolite was dug in prehistoric times.

Wicken Fen is nearby, a wet land reserve and the oldest nature reserve in the country; it was, in 1899, the first tract of land given to the National Trust. As Wicken Fen looks today it is very much as Celia would have seen all the fen country of East Anglia and Lincolnshire. It is a strange kind of place, the ground so lacks consolidation that the working of a piledriver or even a heavy person jumping up and down can be felt by someone standing some distance away. It was a sunny day in autumn, swans were gliding around on the water, the summer visitors had departed and it was quite delightful to make a change from the saddle by squelching through the peat and by listening to the various birds. Originally sedge would have been cut for thatching and peat dug for fuel, but the work is now carried out purely to maintain the character of the fen.

After this pleasant break I saddled up and set off again, taking the metalled road to Little Wilbraham and Great Wilbraham. We passed by the next defence ditch, Fleam Dyke, and carried on to Fulbourn and the Gog Magog Hills. This brought us to the outskirts of Cambridge, which I intended to visit on foot.

I decided to box Rowan home and leave him in his home surroundings while visiting Cambridge and Ely. Having done that the intention was to take him back to Cambridge in the trailer and ride from Cambridge to Ely and west to Hunting-

Windpump, Wicken Fen

don and then northwards to Wansford and Leicester. Having arrived home and having sorted out the accommodation for horse and rider for the next few days, I walked to the paddock adjacent to the house in order to stable Rowan and feed him. To my horror, however, I found him standing looking dejected and unwilling to move. I realised at once that he was very ill and while I encouraged him to the stable and rugged him up, Bill hurried back to the house and called the vet.

As I write these words I find to my surprise that I have literally to relive the agony of those next fourteen hours. Rowan was showing symptoms of acute colic but, after several visits, the vet found that there was nothing that he could do to save him. He had to be put down in his own stable with us there, which should be the end of every horse. Surely that is the least that we can do at the end of their life in view of the years of service and fun that they have given us. A post mortem revealed, as explained in The Introduction, that a tear of the intestinal wall support had occurred for no known reason.

I had always thought Rowan to be one of those horses who would still be doing long distances at the age of 25 but fate had stepped in and decreed otherwise. What more can be said, except that I had ten wonderful years of long distance riding on him to look back on and treasure.

Part IV

An early Journey

Ridden on Cameron in 1991

21

Horses in the Seventeenth Century

It is a pity that Celia says nothing about the type of horse which she and her servants rode, or indeed about the people whom she met while riding. One can speculate on what type of horse she might have ridden by considering the breeds which were known at the time and their characteristics. The horses and ponies in England then were probably as varied as they are today. It was, as stated in an earlier chapter, altogether a time of change and this applied to horses as in other ways. We were at that time not only importing large numbers of horses from Italy and the Iberian peninsula but we were also breeding lighter and faster horses.

Information about horses of the time can be gleaned from various writings including those of the Duke of Newcastle and also from wills and inventories of the period. Another important source of information is from paintings: owners would commission portraits of individual horses but we must remember that it was not until Stubbs studied the anatomy of the horse that we obtained a really accurate representation of the animal. We have only to look at some portraits of the time to see spindly legs and gross bodies which must have been quite inaccurate; however, these pre-Stubbs paintings do serve as a most useful guide. There were, as there are today, various types of horse together with a number of native ponies and we will endeavour to describe the most common types of both in order to obtain an idea of what Celia might have ridden.

From the Middle Ages the all-purpose riding horse had been the palfrey and there are many references to it, especially in the records of the great abbeys of the north of England where many were bred. As far back as the twelfth century these animals were worth twenty shillings or one and a half marks, in today's terms about £375. The breeders of Wensleydale produced ambling palfreys which were reckoned to be second to none and the market charter of Askrigg in Wensleydale was granted as early as 1202 by King John, in consideration of the gift of a palfrey for the king to hunt on. So the palfrey was clearly thought well of and was already then an important breed. Several centuries later, in the seventeenth century, a valuation of the estate of Adam Middleham of Gill, near Aysgarth, included "two bay and eleven gray mares, and one bay nag, and one gray mare, one sanded (bay dun) mare, one gray nagge, one young gray mare and one gray cold stag (yearling colt). The first lot are valued at forty pound for the thirteen, or about three pounds, one shilling and sevenpence each, and the second at eight pounds, six shillings and eightpence for six, or one pound, thirteen shillings and fourpence a head.'' To put these values into today's terms, one should take the pound then as worth £54 today. This breed was completely contemporaneous with Celia as James I was the last monarch to ride a palfrey on public and state occasions; succeeding monarchs rode Neapolitans.

The amble is an artificial gait, easily taught to most short-backed, well-made horses, and indeed a few do it naturally. In the east, where long journeys on horseback were still necessary until recent times, most riders used amblers and anyone who has enjoyed this gait will know how easy it is to sit. Blundervill, an Elizabethan, wrote "... if you take away the ambling horse, you take away the horse for the old man, the rich man, the weak man, nay generally all men's travels...'' In the sixteenth and seventeenth centuries men went around the country training horses to amble. This gait lasted in England from Roman times but, sadly, it has now died out.

The rouncy was a hard trotting cob, the forerunner of today's Welsh Cob or Powys horse. The Welsh cob has probably evolved from the Welsh pony with the infusion of Barb and Andalusian blood, starting in Roman times. In the tenth century the codified laws formed the basis of Welsh law for six centuries and they describe three types of horse: one the palfrey, the second the rowny or sumpter (the packhorse) and the third the working horse. This was a light able-bodied working horse which pulled a sledge. Fifteenth century manuscripts depict the British knight on the destrier, this was the Spanish type of warhorse and from medieval times the knight would need the minimum of three horses to keep him in action day after day. So he would have two destriers and a palfrey for riding, plus a cob or rouncy for the squire to ride while leading the destrier, also a pack horse to carry the knight's armour. The improvement of the Welsh cob was attributed to the Arab stallions brought back to this country by the Crusaders, so the infusion of the Spanish stallions and the Arabs has brought about the modern Welsh cob. It is not surprising, therefore, that one can readily detect the Arab influence in the face of the cob, especially when the horse is excited.

The destrier was a war horse which was used, for instance, in the Norman invasion of 1066 - the very name means ''led by the squire's right hand''. They were cob sized animals of 13.2 - 14.3 hands, clean-limbed, forward going and strong enough to carry a man in chain mail at a gallop into battle. Even bearing in mind that the average height for men was only 5' 6'' in those days, these horses carried a considerable load indeed. In 1505 we read of this breed being larger and heavier, standing at 14.2 - 15.2 hands and capable of carrying about 30 stone, albeit at a trot. Just over a hundred years later, Charles I was noted as having a Spanish charger of 15 - 16 hands, clean limbed and hot blooded.

At the end of the seventeenth century large numbers of Neapolitan horses were being imported into England and these war horses contributed greatly to the reputation of Naples as being one of the finest centres of horse breeding in Europe. They were large animals and gave the appearance of being somewhat ungainly and ill-shaped. Judging from pictures they looked somewhere between a cross of a heavy hunter and a present-day carthorse, and their size can be gauged at well over 15.2 hands. The Neapolitans liked these horses for carriage driving. The Duke of Newcastle commented "I have often heard Neapolitan horses commended, which I think they justly deserve; but those I have seen were all ill-shaped though strong and vigorous".

The term nag was by this time becoming commoner in English usage, it first occurred in English in 1400 and was apparently unknown to Chaucer. It meant an ordinary riding horse and it could have been applied to a palfrey or a rouncy. In some parts of the country farmworkers would, until recently, still talk of the plough horse or carthorse stables on one side of the yard and the nags' stables on the other where the riding horses were kept. Nags were mainly geldings.

The word "hobby" occurs first in Scotland in 1375 and it was a word used to describe the Irish horses at the battle of Carrickfergus. The words "hobby", "hobyn" or "robin" are variations of the word "Robert". Interestingly, the English pet name for Robert in the same period of Dobbin or Dobyn has become a common name for a carthorse. In the sixteenth and seventeenth centuries the English referred to the Shetland pony as the Scotch Hobby and the Connemara pony as the Irish hobby, but later the word was used to describe a lightweight military horse. In Samuel Johnson's Dictionary of 1765 a hobby was described as an Irish or Scottish horse, a pacing horse or a garran (garran being Gaelic for gelding, possibly a highland horse). Hobbies were often found in the stables of the upper classes who liked them because of their tractable nature and easy pace for riding. Incidentally, Henry VIII made regular gifts of hobbies to other rulers, often in return for horses which he had received himself.

A galloway was a small horse of not more than 14 hands very similar to the Welsh cob. It was used not only for riding but also for transport and even in pairs for ploughing. The term galloway was used to define a definite breed of border pony, more active and alert and less docile than the Highland pony.

They stood at about 14 hands and were well put together, often brown in colour with dark legs and near black hooves which were very tough. They had an easy and rapid gait with great staying power and could ''run'' twelve to fifteen miles without breaking pace. There are recorded instances of such staying power: in 1754 a Mr Corker's galloway went a hundred miles a day for three successive days over the Newmarket course without the slightest distress. Another galloway belonging to a Mr Sinclair of Kirkby Lonsdale performed at Carlisle the amazing feat of a thousand miles in a thousand hours. A certain Rowland Challoner of Sheffield died in 1713 and in his stable he had "..four little galloways with four old pack saddles and surcingles, wanties and panniers for coal carriage worth £6.2.0...'' This type of evidence is rare and normally inventories will say no more than ''mares'', ''geldings'', etc. Defoe describes the Galloway ".. These horses are remarkable for being good pacers, strong easy goers, hardy, gentle, well broken and above all they never tire ...''

Another breed of the time was the roadster or Norfolk horse: it was a trotting horse peculiar to the East Anglian region. It was similar to the Welsh cob and references are known back to King Stephen's time, when the trotter appeared on his seal. The other one that is known to most people is the horse ridden by the reeve in Chaucer's "Canterbury Tales" : "...she was a good mare and a dapple grey cob...". These horses were very popular in the seventeenth and eighteenth centuries and they were used for trotting races, indeed the Norfolk roadster prior to 1700, that is in Celia's time, carried the post. They were known for their soundness of consitution, hard legs and speed and endurance. These horses were capable of travelling long distances and quite an unusual feat was to be able to trot at 15-16 miles/hour carrying an average sized man. They were often roan in colour. My own horse Rowan which I rode for part of my ride was in fact a roan and could trot over a distance at 15 miles/hour when we paced him. I do wonder whether he could have been a descendant of the Norfolk horse as the details of his breeding were not known.

Also in the West Country, in later years, Celia comments about the great many horses passing with packs and returning loaded with coal. The charge, she said, was twelve pence a horse load, the load being two bushels. Another reference to carrying coal was to unloading ships with coal at Bridgewater whence it was taken to Bristol, again each horse carrying two bushels. At Exeter they unloaded serges from ships and the horses took this to Topshun (Topsham) about four miles distant; she saw the carriers entering the town with their loaded horses as they brought the serges from the looms to the fulling mills. She also saw little ponies being used in the West Country and refers to these as Cornish Canelys: they were well made and strong and would trip along lightly on a stony road without injuring themselves, whereas on these roads Celia was complaining that her horses' shoes wore up quickly and fell off.

When Celia was in Devon she saw the harvest being brought in on horses' backs with crooks of wood like yokes on either side of each horse and with a person on either side supporting the load. She met scores of horses transporting the harvest in this way. These little horses were called Canelles, presumably the same type as mentioned earlier although no trace of such a breed can be found today. According to Richard Carew in 1602 there were ponies in Cornwall that were hardy bred, coarsely fed, low of stature, quick in travel and able enough to prove serviceable in a rough and hill country. These ponies, accustomed to living in inhospitable conditions and to fending for themselves, were suitable animals for small farmers to breed, also they were hardy, active and sure-footed and were in demand from the mid-sixteenth century onwards. In the Lake District on her Great Journey she said that the ways were too narrow for coaches and horses with panniers were used. Some of these panniers were open and some closed and they were used to carry hay, lime and dung; Kendal at the time was full of such horses carrying packs.

We do not have accurate descriptions of what pack horses were because they were of varying size and breed. We do know that in the eighteenth century small Welsh horses were used because they were very sure footed and that the carrying of packs was often a part-time occupation which would be taken up by farmers, tradespeople and others at certain times. Carriers, as distinct from pack ponies, went by day only because of the danger of travelling at night due to highwaymen, the bad state of the roads and the lack of signposting. Although Celia does not refer to the horses which they rode she does make a number of references to the pack horses of the time. They tended to be rather harsh, short-gaited horses and ponies which would be uncomfortable to ride over long distances. Again in Devon, where the land had been enclosed and the ways were too narrow for coach and waggons, she notes that they used pack ponies to carry corn in panniers and loaded it high and tied it on with cords. On a journey to Bath in 1687 near Berkeley she comments on a deep clay way which was five miles long and had a narrow causeway, so narrow that a coach could hardly pass along and it was made for pack horses only.

Turning now to other breeds of riding horse, in the book "Perfection of Horsemanship" by Nicholas Morgan, 1609, he arranges breeds in order of popularity in England. The first was the Arabian, then the Thessalian, the Neapolitan, the Barbary, the Turkey and the Spanish Andalusian.

In the early part of the seventeenth century there were no English bred Barbs, the word coming from "Barbary" although Berber is the correct term. They were only half breeds, since the Moors, in common with the Turks and Arabs, would not sell their mares abroad: this meant that we had no pure bred Barbs in this country. The Barb was at first used as a racehorse and was not thought of as a conveyance for either the middle aged or the middle class. These horses originated from Morocco and had a height of 14 - 15 hands; their history can be traced back to 800 AD. The Barb had a considerable influence on the Andalusian and the Spanish horse and is an extraordinarily hard and docile animal which can live on small quantities of poor quality food. It is essentially a riding horse and an older breed than the Arab. Its conformation is ideal for tackling mountainous and difficult terrain. It has a convex face, a high wither and a short back with deeply sloping croup; it is rather upright in stance with small hard hooves. It originally had no Arab blood because the Arab breed did not exist before the time of Christ. There is another Barb, the Libyan Barb: this horse was popular with the Romans as being extremely hardy, tough and sound. It is probable, though, that the breed declined and by the middle of the seventeenth century was already becoming inferior due to overpopularity.

The origin of the Arab horse is unknown but it is thought to be a descendant of the Tarpan and the Central Asiatic horses. There were also Persian horses of this type, depicted around 2000 BC, which were used for riding and for war chariots and the Persians maintain that the Persian Arab is the oldest known domesticated breed in the world. The earliest records of horses in southern Arabia appear in about 400 AD, when two hundred horses were sent by Constant I to the Yemeni. When Mahomet came into power in the seventh century he realised the value of these horses, not only for his own army but for the Arab people in general and the horse became part of their social and religious world. It was from that time that the Arab became pure bred.

For centuries the Bedouins have taken the greatest care in the selection of their stock; unusually the mares are selected for their endurance during long hunts covering great distances across sandy plains, while the stallions are chosen for their beauty, conformation and intelligence. The Arab has the bulk of its weight forward on its forehand so that it is an ideal horse for prolonged cantering over endless flat plains in the desert. The Arab was created under hostile conditions, with burning sun by day and freezing cold by night. In order to fortify these horses they were often fed on camel's milk and dried meat in the dry season. To this day the Arabs are renowned for their endurance capabilities and are sought by many riders for this quality. The height of the Arab is between 14 and 15.2 hands and they are mostly whole colours. They are distinctive in that they have one fewer pair of ribs than most other horses.

The Andalusian was developed from the Barb and the Arab mated with the native Spanish horses and in the Middle Ages it had a considerable influence on the breeds of European horses. These horses today are elegant and very active and tend to be over 15 hands.

The Civil War in the seventeenth century made a large impact on the breeding of horses and the large, slower horses - warbles - were then sought out. This horse had been losing ground in England during the period 1558 - 1625 but then these large horses were required as troop horses and even as officers' chargers, although this was to the detriment of light horse breeding.

It is recorded that a large number of horses in the period 1684 - 1720 were purchased in markets such as Market Bosworth in Leicestershire and Boughton Green in Northamptonshire by Londoners, in the main by three large horse dealers. The sales or fairs nearer London also fulfilled the large demand for horses in the London region.

In the late seventeenth century the upper classes were concentrating on breeding their own quality horses, keeping the best for their own use and improving the lines by importing Barbs, Arabs and other types. Sir Roger Pratt of Rystone Hall in Norfolk prided himself on being self-sufficient in saddle and cart horses. These breeders clearly kept the best stock for themselves and sold off the surplus. There is a recorded comment from 1691 "... take care not to be overstocked ... keep few idle horses ..."

Although Celia would have owned her own and her servants' horses, those too poor to hire a horse for themselves would sometimes hire one together with a companion. One would ride and the other would run or both would ride the same horse together or they would have recourse to carriers, one person sitting above the load with their legs horizontal on top of panniers. This mode of travel was still in use in the eighteenth century.

Small scale horse breeding was generally for the immediate locality and horses were either sold privately to friends and neighbours or at nearby markets and fairs. In Staffordshire, in the late seventeenth century, surviving toll-books show that three quarters of the sellers and more than two thirds of the buyers lived within a 10 mile radius. At Penkridge there was a recognised centre of horse selling and this market is where the better off would come to buy their horses; horses from the Continent would even be imported to this fair. By the late sixteenth and early seventeenth centuries there was such pressure on grazing grounds that one would have specific areas in the country for breeding horses and other areas for rearing. Small horses and ponies were bred in the hilly areas of the western Pennines and also in Wales; it is from these areas today that the native ponies still come.

Horses in the seventeenth and eighteenth centuries had a social as well as an economic value, since at all levels of society they were regarded as status symbols. The upper classes could display wealth by the purchase of expensive horses and at a lower level the purchase of a horse could raise the owner's standing in his community. The possession of a horse made the owner independent and allowed him to travel farther and quicker and to expand his social sphere. In many villages the division between horse owners and others must have made a clear social distinction between, in modern terminology, the haves and the have-nots. Indeed, the position of the motor car in society today is analagous to that of the horse then.

There is a valuable document in the accounts of Sir Richard Newdigate of Warwickshire, a horse enthusiast. In 1691, "... lest my wife, son or relations should think I overprize (overprice) my horses I will set down the names and prizes (prices) ..." Some excerpts follow: "... Age 14, Old Turk, price 200 pounds, colour bright bay Age 16, Old Wilks, price 150 pounds, colour chesnut, two white legs Age 6, Strawberry, price 100 pounds, colour sandy grey ..."

Towards the end of the seventeenth century, England was no longer dependent upon importing horses from abroad and by the close of the century the export of horses had begun. The upper classes were turning their interests towards horse racing rather than riding for utilitarian reasons and this gave impetus for growth to places like Newmarket and Chester.

The story of the horse in this country is a long and complex one and it is only by studying the background to this subject that one can begin to appreciate what type of horse Celia might have used.

22

Newton Tony to Broughton Castle

I felt that my ride was incomplete without visiting Celia's birthplace at Newton Tony in Wiltshire, not only because of its significance as the starting point of the Celia Fiennes story but also because many of her rides began there. Some of the early ones were made with her mother and may have been made by coach rather than on horseback, but that is a point of detail which I discounted. Thus I determined to recreate a journey to one of the other family homes of Broughton Castle. So I found myself setting off in Holy Week from a point near Newton Tony (the spelling has changed of recent years from Toney) to ride into the village. I was originally planning to ride down the portway, one of the main Roman roads in the country, however this runs alongside a railway line and I decided that discretion was the better part of valour. My previous experience with trains rattling close to Cameron had resulted in disaster and I had no wish to repeat the experience at the beginning of a ride on a fresh horse.

As it turned out, Cameron was very fresh and eager to get going and was attempting to spook at every shadow or imaginary shadow, birds twittering in the hedge and so on. The best thing to do was to trot on for a mile or so, giving him time to settle. This is all right on your home ground where you know the geography of the landscape intimately but when you have to read your map you have to go slower and relate your route to it. Unfortunately, despite my precautions, Cameron managed to ditch me within the first ten minutes; even after several years of long distance riding he can still be a difficult ride. However I landed pretty well on my feet, remounted and rode to Celia's birthplace of Newton Tony.

Sadly, Nathaniel Fiennes, Celia's father, never made his peace with Charles II and after his death his widow was still upholding the cause of Protestant dissent; she appointed the Rev John Cross as her private chaplain after he was deprived of his benefice for nonconformity. In 1676 the village of Newton Tony harboured 26 nonconformists to 84 Anglicans. In 1709 the house was sold and Celia was one of the signatories to the deed. She says nothing about the village, only that the ways when wet were slippery because of the chalk downs and that it was ideal country for racing, hunting and coursing. She uses the term "champion" - this was first used in the sixteenth century to describe landscapes that differed from those of the early Middle Ages. The champion regions were the areas where the agriculture was organised in the classic open-field system. The settlement pattern was one of nucleated villages and the arable land was in numerous small strips. These were usually less than an acre in size and were grouped together in bundles known as shotts or furlongs, the word ''furlong'' of course being derived from ''long furrow''; furlongs were arranged in two, three or four huge fields and the strips or furlongs were not hedged. Villages were often isolated amongst vast open plains of agricultural land, each farmer's strips were scattered across the fields in the village and there had to be a communal rotation between crops and grazing. An interesting point is that where the champion lands existed the roads tended to be straighter, whereas in the woodland areas they tended to be winding and bounded by high hedges and banks. In many parts of the country one finds the woodland and champion landscapes side by side.

The only memorial to Celia is at her own request: her name and dates of birth and death are added to her father's monument in the church and, interestingly, it gives the names of both Cecilia and Celia. Sadly I found the church rather dark and depressing although well cared for: the fact that it had suffered at the hands of the Victorian restorers was certainly a contributory factor.

However, the part of the village close to the church is attractive with houses and a farm fronting onto a small river which, because of the low rainfall over the last two years or so, was completely dry. The scene was enlivened, though, by the arrival of a lady from the house opposite the church who carefully descended one river bank and then ascended the other to engage me in conversation. She was interested to know something of the reason for my visit and immediately responded to the name of Celia Fiennes. I was delighted that she was not forgotten and I told the lady of my various rides recreating those of Celia.

I bade her farewell and then we headed north: there was a choice of at least two ways open to me. One was to use the Old Marlborough Road which is a very long length of bridleway and the other was to dodge around the army camps at Tidworth. I chose the latter largely because my son Philip lives not far away and by this means it was easier for him to accompany me for part of the way on a mountain bike. As we progressed northwards beyond Ludgershall, crossed the Blackmoor Downs and then climbed up to Chute Causeway, I was delighted by the beautiful scenery. My pleasure was enhanced even further by the lovely weather and by the continuing climb which, combined with the mileage which we had by now covered, had a steadying effect on my horse.

We stopped for a drink at a pub a mile or so short of crossing the Causeway and I was fascinated to learn from the publican that some months previously a party of riders had passed that way who had ridden from the Midlands on bridleways and were planning to go to Scotland in a similar way. It was thrilling to feel oneself part of a band of riders whom one rarely meets on one's travels but of whom one learns from time to time by word of mouth or by reading. After leaving the pub we went on to cross the Causeway which is interesting in that it is a Roman road which, because of the steep hills in the area on which hill forts are perched, deviated from the usual direct line. The Causeway was not a Roman military road; had it been so it would have probably gone straight into the valley of Hippenscombe but this road was a civil one which linked the agricultural cornlands of Hampshire with the Gloucestershire Cotswolds. Christopher Taylor states that it was a road for wheeled traffic and possibly for carrying heavy goods so steep slopes had to be avoided at all costs. Incidentally, the road looks as if it is curved but it is in fact made up of nine short alignments, each between three quarters and one and a quarter miles in length.

The steepness of the road was brought home to me fully when we descended into the valley: it really was incredibly steep and reminded me of Derbyshire, the county where a friend once described the hills as "real humdingers". Because Cameron was not fully fit I decided to lead him and Philip pushed his bike. I was just about to mount when Philip cried "Look out, llamas ahead". I realised, of course, that he meant the animals and not Tibetan priests and I continued to lead a very excited, snorting and prancing horse forwards and sideways past these strange creatures. Having negotiated past the beasts Philip then called out "Watch it, one of them is galloping up behind". With a further snorting and prancing by Cameron we finally managed to clear the hazard. Ideally I should have remounted and ridden him back and forth for half an hour until he took no notice of the llamas, but time was pressing and I was conscious that we were hoping to reach our stabling by about 5pm.

We climbed out of the valley with Philip pedalling up the inclines of 1 in 4 or 5 in the lowest of his 15 gears and Cameron plodding on without complaint. We went on for about half and hour but I found that I could not then relate the track to the Ordnance Survey map. I asked Philip's opinion and we quickly came to the conclusion that we must have gone wrong at the llamas. So we had no alternative but to retrace our steps past them again, with Philip muttering "Never give Mother a map". We found a helpful tractor driver who put us right and we continued on the right track for the rest of that day. If I had not been distracted by an excitable horse at a critical point we would undoubtedly not have taken the wrong turn but I was consoled to some extent by the fact that the track which we took did not appear on the Ordnance Survey map. We arrived at our night's stabling an hour later than we intended but we were relieved to find a most professional set-up there and in no time Cameron was ensconced in a large and modern stable and I was installed in the manor house, complete with a cheery fire in the room and plenty of hot water in the adjacent bathroom.

Next day we continued towards Hungerford using part of the Inkpen Ridgeway. The only people we met in the early stages were trailriders, all of whom were extremely courteous and stopped and turned their engines off as we passed. There were gates to open and close along the way and, sadly, only one could be manipulated from Cameron's back. I reflected once again how short-sighted it is of landowners to expect their gates to be closed after passage and yet not provide a type which can be operated from horseback. The views from the ridge were quite stunning and I was tempted to ride the ridge to the far end and not strike northwards as I had planned. The Inkpen Ridgeway carries on eastwards and joins up with the North Downs Way, the range of chalk hills eventually finishing at the English Channel at Dover.

I rode past the sign of the Combe Gibbet which is marked on the Ordnance Survey map. It may still be there but if so I missed it, all I saw was some motor cyclists messing about up and down some short steep slopes and charging towards me at one stage. However, one of their number drew their attention to me and, thankfully, they turned their engines off at once. Afterwards I discovered that the mound which the motor cyclists had been using for their games was a barrow but I guess they could not have been expected to know that. How lucky the horse riders in this area are, with their miles and miles of ridges and other trackways to ride: the minor hassle with the motor cyclists pales into insignificance beside this enormous virtue.

Interestingly, the Inkpen Ridgeway reaches heights of as much as 950 feet, which gives some indication of the severity of the hills which we had tackled. Just beyond the Gibbet is Walbury Hill, an Iron Age fort which is the highest point of the chalk in the country. I decided to keep to my planned route and we then had to drop down some 800 feet into Hungerford.

The name of the town means quite simply the ford where people are hungry. In bygone days it was on the coaching routes and in Paterson's Roads of 1841 it is described as consisting "... principally of one long street which is situated on marshy soil on the banks of the Kennet and is watered by two separate streams of that river. Near the town centre is the market house and shambles and over the latter is a large room where the inhabitants meet for the despatch of business; in this room a curious relick of antiquity is preserved, denominated the Hungerford horn, which was given with a charter to the town by John of Gaunt''. Hungerford lodged Prince William of Orange on his way to London from Torbay with a force of Ango-Dutch troops in the lead-up to "The Glorious Revolution". On that Thursday, 6 December 1694, the town became crowded with troops; the northern lords brought with them hundreds of cavalry and from there they marched to London. All this happened several years before Celia's long rides but after her original visit to the town.

Hungerford is where the Kennet & Avon canal, built a hundred and fifty years after Celia's rides, diverges from the valley to climb over the watershed into the Vale of Pewsey. What a change it was from the quietness and the sound of the wind of the hills to come down into the bustle of a town once again. The streets were full of holidaymakers on this Good Friday and the traffic was nose to tail. There were pleasure boats on the river and the canal and the whole scene was one of intense activity of people enjoying themselves. Celia describes the town as being famous for large crawfish, great quantities of which were taken from the river there, but whether they are still to be found I do not know.

We soon left the crowds behind, however, and continued on our way northwards by byway and bridleway. I had to cross the M4 and I decided to do it by means of the bridleway which passes through The Holt estate. About a mile before the motorway I could hear the roar of the traffic, building up for the Easter holiday, and my heart was sinking lower and lower. However, when I reached the bridge Cameron just took one sideways look at the traffic and then plodded over like an old horse without a glance to either side. He is a funny creature. We continued along bridleways to Lambourn, ascending and descending through woodland and open downland. The town is, of course, along with Newmarket and Middleham one of the great centres of racehorse training in the country, and as we came down from the hills above the town the neatly laid out stable yards were clearly evident.

The next morning we continued our journey northwards and rode for a short distance along The Ridgeway. I reflected that it was nearly sixteen years since I had ridden that route before, which was on my old horse Rowan. The detail of that journey was still fresh in my mind, the whole thing had been such an adventure and so enjoyable. The Ridgeway seemed, for some reason, to light Cameron up and one would think that he had not been ridden for weeks. He was equally hard to sit at a trot or canter as he would, with no warning at all, veer off to the left or right. I was lucky to stay in the saddle, as I mentioned earlier he really is a funny horse.

On this part of The Ridgeway is Wayland's Smithy, a neolithic tomb with folklore associations with Wayland, the smith of the old Saxon gods. The local legend has it that if you leave your horse by the tomb with a coin on the lintel stone you can return to find that it has been shod. A mile farther on is Uffingham Castle and White Horse Hill: the White Horse is the most famous of all the hill figures in Europe and is best seen from the train. The figure is 360 feet long by 160 feet high and is well proportioned with the appearance of galloping uphill. Hardly anything is known about its origin, but it is believed to date from the first century AD, although it could be as much as one or two thousand years older. Celia mentions it, saying that it is "... cutt out the shape off a horse in perfect proportions, in broad wayes, and is seen a great distance very plaine ..".

A short way away, although not visited on this journey, is the Blowing Stone, a block of sarsen which is riddled with holes like a piece of Gruyere cheese which can be blown into to emit a deep trumpet-like note. Legend has it that King Arthur used it to rally his troops.

It should be appreciated, of course, that all these ridge ways are prehistoric roads which enabled early man to avoid the difficulty and danger of low-lying and boggy ground. Although I wished to spend longer in the area I realised that unless I pushed on I would not make my night's stabling at a reasonable time. We descended the steep hill and then went by a bridleway north westwards. It had obviously been cleared recently; luckily the weather was dry, otherwise it would probably by the look of it have had what Celia would have described as a muddy bottom.

A number of new bridleway gates had been erected but none of them could be operated from the back of Cameron. One set which caused me a particular problem was mounted on either side of a narrow bridge with no room at all to turn Cameron while I tried to operate the gates. In the end I decided to lead him rather than keep clambering off and on. The rest of our ride to Coleshill was uneventful. The only difficulty was crossing the A420; the visibility for horseriders was virtually nil but, it being the holiday weekend, I thought there would be relatively light traffic but how wrong I was. When I reached Coleshill I was asked by a local person how on earth I had managed to cross. When eventually I arrived home after the ride I learnt from the newspapers which had accumulated while I was away that several people had been killed in a car crash near that spot not long after I had gone over.

We ended up in the village of Coleshill, hoping to see the house which Celia describes in great detail with its avenues, fine walks and rows of trees, together with gardens with flowering trees and apricots and other fruit trees. The house in the late seventeenth century was newly built in stone; the entrance was an ascent of several steps into a hall which went up three floors. It had a gallery and large rooms well and fashionably furnished; the house was built by Sir Roger Pratt, who consulted with Inigo Jones, between 1650 and 1652. Sadly I had not realised that this National Trust property had been burnt down in 1954 as the result of a workman's carelessness. However, the view of the village perched on a hill some mile or so from the stables was delightful. It was less pleasant to learn that the church was shut up, with the appearance of being redundant and neglected, owing to continuing vandalism.

The next day I continued northwards through the Vale of the White Horse and reflected how well the ride had gone thus far. I decided to make a short detour up Akeman Street, once one of the four major roads in the country, and then ride up close to the Wychwood Forest. This was one of the old hunting forests and a deer park remains as evidence of it at nearby Cornbury Park. From the Ordnance Survey map one can see indications of how much larger the forest was as little as a hundred years ago by the names of lodges, Chase Farm, Kingstanding Farm and so on. Indeed I later discovered that one of the bridleways which I used formed part of the pre-Conquest boundary of Witney. From the bridleway I could see the avenues which would have been used to drive deer down to be hunted and it was one of the many occasions on my ride when history came very much alive. Wychwood Forest survived until the deforestation which took place by Act of Parliament as recently as 1857, but this area is still the woodiest part of Oxfordshire and, interestingly, Leafield which I rode through was first recorded as La Felde which probably means "old clearing" or "lawn of pasture" and in 1213 it was known as Field Town.

I carried on partly along the newly created Oxfordshire Way and then northwards, skirting the town of Chipping Norton on the way. Later that day occurred the one skirmish. A man was sitting quietly fishing for trout and he was casting his line back and forth; Cameron suddenly sensed great danger, made even more intense by the appearance of a terrifying harrow lying half hidden in the grass. He quickly went into reverse at high speed and I started to turn him in a circle in order to drive him forward. Half-way round the circle though he put in two enormous bucks and managed to unseat me. I called out to the angler to hold on until I was past. This he did but by this time Cameron had reverted to his sedate horse mode and continued as if nothing had happened. The angler must have thought that his sport was much less hazardous than mine. The fact that I had ridden that day for as long as five hours had apparently had no effect on the horse whatsoever.

I continued northwards and headed towards Broughton as there was still some daylight left. On the last three miles I encountered the only navigational problem of the day: the bridleway was completely undefined with no waymarking and it was a question of crossing one grass field after another. If I could have seen a gate or a gap I might have known where to aim for but I could not even see the far side of the fields. The only method of navigation was by the contours, not an easy matter as even on a horse like Cameron who allows one to stop to read a map one is never completely still. I could not even follow the hoofprints left by other riders as prints abounded everywhere but as we progressed I found a large field with jumps in it and this explained the profusion of hoofprints. Whether by luck or judgment we emerged at the right spot at Lower Tadmarton where we were to stay the night. It was just as well, at one point I really did wonder whether I would have to retrace my steps and go about six miles round by the road. I had had a very long day in the saddle and was relieved to reach my night's halt. Cameron, however, could obviously have gone on quite happily for several more hours.

His stable, the accommodation and the meal at a nearby pub all earned five star rating. One thing which particularly pleased me was that the pub had no outside lighting, unlike almost every other hostelry today; as we approached it was for all the world as Celia might have seen it, with glimpses of people eating and drinking seen through the tiny windows in the middle of a village in almost total darkness.

The next day I visited the nearby Rollright Stones of which Celia makes no mention. These form a stone circle which was erected about four thousand years ago during the Bronze Age: folklore has it that that no one has ever been able to count them accurately. The King's Stone, which is separated from the circle by the Jurassic Way, said by some to be the oldest road in the country, is said by ancient belief to go down to the stream to drink when the clock strikes midnight.

I also took the opportunity of visiting the Four Shires Stone and was thrilled to find that it is still there just as Celia saw it on one of her rides; it marks the boundaries between Gloucestershire, Oxfordshire, Warwickshire and Worcestershire. Sadly, though probably necessarily, it has metal railings around it for protection. It marks a useful landmark on Celia's journeys as it enables us to pinpoint precisely the route which she took on that particular ride.

I now had the last short lap to complete to the family home at Broughton Castle. I rode along the byway to Fulling Mill Farm just outside the boundary of the park and climbed round on the western side, then met up with my husband at Woadmill Farm, another reminder with the previous farm of past industries in the area.

I had earlier visited Broughton Castle without Cameron during the Warwick to St Albans section of the ride and had received a friendly welcome from Lord

& Lady Saye & Sele. The name Sele, incidentally, comes from that of a small Kentish village near Sevenoaks because at one time the family owned nearby Knole of Sackville fame. On the occason of that visit it was an exciting moment to see for the first time Celia's diary in her own hand. It also gave me great pleasure to wander about the Castle, which is kept very much as a family home, and to see the reconstructed knot garden. The public are not regimented in any way and are able to choose their own route through the house. To see many parts of the house as they would have appeared in Celia's time was a rewarding experience indeed; sadly though there is no portrait of Celia, although there are portraits of many of her relations.

The Gatehouse, Broughton Castle

Broughton Castle was built about the year 1300 and was completely reconstructed in 1554. During the seventeenth century the Castle was the scene of meetings called to plan opposition to the King's government. They were held under the pretext of the Providence Island Company, formed to colonise certain islands in the Caribbean. It appears probable that the Civil War was virtually planned there and during the War William and his four sons actively supported the Parliamentarians; he raised in the Banbury area a regiment of bluecoats and four troops of horse who fought in the nearby Battle of Edgehill in 1642. Banbury was indeed said to be the most Puritanical town in England.

As I looked now at the lovely grey house on the far side of the park I reflected on how well the last few days' ride had gone. All the bridleways had been open, even if some had not been easy to find, and the stabling and accommodation had all been good, indeed very good. Riding up from Newton Tony to Broughton I had been able to gain a new insight into the structure of the country as I crossed from ridge to ridge and saw a cross-section of the geology of the country. I was very conscious of the fact that I had ridden for about a thousand miles in total in seeking to recreate the Northern Journey of Celia Fiennes and part of the East Anglian section of the Great Journey. The more that I become involved with Celia and her journeys the greater is my desire to set off on a re-creation of the Great Journey around England and also on some more of the shorter journeys.

Part V

Notes on the Ride including mileages

Some places to visit

Bibliography

Notes on the Ride

Since childhood I had read every available book on horseback journeys and it was in this connection that I originally heard of Celia Fiennes. What I needed to do was to study "The Journals of Celia Fiennes" but I had the greatest difficulty in obtaining them. Then one day in 1976 I heard from Mrs Kent, the secondhand bookseller in nearby Framlingham, that she had found a copy of the 1947 edition and naturally this was a very exciting moment. Later I purchased a copy of the 1981 edition when it was published but I was disappointed to find that it omitted Celia's mileages so that I have continued to use the 1947 edition as my "bible". I read both many times and frequently dipped into them subsequently so that, when I came to plan my re-creation of the ride, I was already well steeped in them. Indeed, I almost felt as if I had come to know Celia as a person.

My next step was to borrow from the library the Ordnance Survey maps covering the ride to see whether my idea was practicable, bearing in mind that I wanted the route to be on quiet lanes and bridleways and not on busy metalled roads. I had no intention, even on my original horse Rowan who was completely traffic-proof, of riding into the centres of large towns and conurbations. This preparatory stage, which included a great deal of measuring distances, took many months of winter evenings with the floor covered with maps.

Once I was sure that the ride was a practicable proposition I then had to begin to plan it in detail. This involved dividing it into day-long sections and looking at every bridleway in detail, studying the road and water crossings with a magnifier to ensure that any potential hazard had been allowed for. The mammoth task of trying to locate stabling was then begun. This was a long process of telephoning possible places which I had identified from lists of stables, riding schools, yellow pages, guides and any other source of information which I could lay my hands on. Once this stage was complete I then set about finding accommodation for my husband (as backup support) and me near enough to the stabling for me to feed and look after my horse. This was a little easier than finding stabling but it still took time.

Eventually these preliminaries were complete but the master plan had to be modified a number of times according to circumstance as the ride progressed. A horse is not a machine and one cannot always cover the ground in precisely the way as planned: a lost shoe, a fall, a blocked bridleway or any other unforeseen problem can completely spoil a day's or even a week's ride. I knew that for most of the time I would be riding in unknown territory and that anything might happen to affect my plans.

The horse on which I began the ride and on which I intended to complete the whole ride was Rowan, a red roan cob with a flaxen mane and tail. His appearance was very striking but his breeding was not known, although he was believed to be a Welsh Cob. With the passage of time, however, and partly as a result of writing this book, I have come to believe that perhaps he was a descendant of the Norfolk Horses. He stood at 15.1 hands and weighed around 500 kg. I had owned him for ten years and he was a veteran of several previous long rides, including The Ridgeway, The South Downs Way and other rides across various counties, mainly in East Anglia. When we started the ride he was a "young" seventeen year old and, as mentioned in the text, he was five gaited and a fast walker and trotter. One could easily cover over thirty miles a day on him.

The rest of the journey was ridden on Marbeck Cameron, a deep chesnut half-bred Welsh Cob/Thoroughbred by the HIS King Willow out of the Welsh Cob Rowen Morwenna. Cameron stands at over 16 hands and weighs around 600 kg. I bought him as a foal in 1980 from Mr Dick Monks, then a veterinary surgeon practising in North Suffolk, intending the horse as a replacement for Rowan. As commented on in the text, Rowan died earlier than I could reasonably have expected and there was consequently a gap of several years before I could resume my ride, as Cameron was at that time too young and immature for such a venture.

My practice regarding feeding is to carry my own hard feed so that there is little change of diet and this minimises the possibility of colic. I carry the proprietary product Horse Hage for emergency use rather than hay because it is of consistent quality, easy to transport and also, not an unimportant point, horses thrive on it. If stables en route have hay of acceptable quality, then of course I use that. I mix the hard feed (concentrates to supplement grass and hay) with alfalfa (lucerne). For the record I should mention that I use Bailey's cereal and nuts as hard feed. I did once give Cameron high protein feed but with disastrous results: it went straight to his head and made him virtually unmanageable. Unless it is raining very hard I always graze Cameron at a lunch break for at least half an hour and also at the end of the day for as long as practicable , and my practice was the same with Rowan. I let Cameron snatch grass while I pause to study the map or open a gate but never while I am riding along.

I often used to ride Rowan in a Kimblewick bit because of his immense strength and rather hard mouth, but Cameron I rode in an eggbutt snaffle. On both horses I used the same saddle, a general purpose deep-seated spring tree. I found the Cottage Craft girth to be ideal because it is easy to keep clean and the shaped version never rubs. Before I started the long ride with Cameron I had various problems with numnahs: he is very thin skinned and after riding he would often come up in bumps which were believed to be the result of allergies. I decided to use only pure soap for washing his girths and numnahs and this appeared to solve the problem. Later I was recommended to try a German Sympatex plastic numnah which is quite stiff, moulds to the horse's back and does not ruck in use. It is quite remarkable and is recommended to any rider who wishes to spend long hours in the saddle, especially if they have a horse with a sensitive back.

Under the bridle I keep an American light nylon head-collar and long rope permanently in position: this enables me to tie Cameron up at any time, for instance while opening and closing difficult gates, or to to slip his bridle off readily to graze him at any opportunity. We carry two 25 litre carriers of water and buckets in the backup vehicle but I offer him water at every opportunity en route, at fords, troughs, streams, clean puddles and so on. It has to be appreciated that some stables will leave only two buckets of water with the horse at night, which is insufficient for a horse doing long-distance work in hot weather.

I carry in my saddlebag a bandage and a hoof-pick and also an Equiboot lest Cameron loses a shoe. The current day's maps, Ordnance Survey 1:50 000 or 1:25 000 in difficult terrain such as Derbyshire or Yorkshire, I carry in a transparent map case round my neck together with a compass and a whistle. (Since completing the ride and following a near disaster in the Yorkshire Dales I also carry a long rope as well.) Ideally one should probably use the 1:25 000 scale at all times but on a long ride this would call for such a large quantity of maps - on this ride I ''rode across'' as many as thirty 1:50 000 Ordnance Survey maps - that I have compromised by using the smaller scale ones wherever possible. In the backup vehicle I carry a spare set of horse shoes, a spare bridle and girth and a long rope but I have fortunately never had recourse to any of them.

I wear either stretch cord or summer light-weight jodhpurs or riding trousers with a Newmarket boot or rubber riding boot. Long boots were necessary in the wet summers of 1983 & 1988 because of the times when one had to dismount into mud at gateways and so on or to wade through water. In any case they do give some measure of protection from trees and shrubs although they can be hot on occasions, but this is something one has to accept. (When I have ridden in Southern Spain I have resorted to a lace-up canvas boot which is something of the best of both worlds.)

When I am riding in hilly areas or on open moorland on my own I wear a bright red sweater or other garment so that I can be spotted readily in the event of difficulty, and on roads I wear a high visibility vest for safety reasons. I also carry a personal alarm which emits a high-pitched shriek so that I can call for assistance should I fall into a ditch or encounter similar difficulty. I now always wear a riding hat to BS 4472 although I did at one time not always wear a hat when riding Rowan.

With Rowan I would often go off all day and meet up with my back-up at a pre-arranged point at the end of the day. Rowan was completely traffic-proof and I was confident that I could tackle any problem on him whether I was on a major trunk road, a bridleway or any other type of route. What he could not go over he would crawl under. Cameron has a very different temperament; he is not good in traffic and is likely to veer off a defined line if a bird twitters or whatever or to swing round and dive out of a situation at the last minute. He is not an easy horse to ride but he has improved out of all recognition over the last year or so. The plus points are that he will tackle any bridleway conditions, wade into deep water, settle down in strange stables and always clear up all his feed. Furthermore, after riding him for six or seven days consecutively he will look as if he has just stepped out of the stable on the first day. The ride enabled him to mature and he finished it a very different horse. On either horse I never rode for more than seven days without a break.

I hope that this book will encourage other riders to see England from the back of a horse. It is still possible, towards the end of the twentieth century, to ride long distances across country interspersed with only a few metalled roads. All that one requires are a sense of adventure, a sound horse, competence in horsemastership and riding and an ability to read a map quickly and accurately. Underlying all these is the necessary determination never to give up. At times the going can be tough but the rewards are tremendous.

Approximate horse mileages

Cheshunt - Bishop's Stortford	18 miles
Bishop's Stortford - Littlebury	19
Littlebury - Cambridge via Wool Street	21
Cambridge - Huntingdon	25
Huntingdon - Warmington via Stilton	30
Warmington - Wansford	9
Wansford - Caldecott	22
Caldecott - Leicester	22
Leicester - Stamford	not ridden
Stamford - Colsterworth	22
Colsterworth - Grantham	15
Grantham - Lincoln	34
Lincoln - Newark	not ridden
Newark - Nottingham	8
Scarborough - Newton-on-Rawcliffe	29
Newton-on-Rawcliffe - Easingwold	35
Easingwold - Nidd (for Ripon)	28
Ripon - Knaresborough - Harrogate	15
Harrogate - York	25
York - Tadcaster	12
Tadcaster - Wentbridge	15
Wentbridge - Worksop	47
Worksop - Mansfield	15
Chesterfield - Chatsworth - Haddon - Bakewell	20
Bakewell - Buxton	14
Buxton - Ashbourne (via Tissington Trail)	26
Ashbourne - Uttoxeter	47
Uttoxeter - Lichfield	29

Lichfield - Warwick	not ridden
Warwick - Daventry	17
Daventry - Stony Stratford	32
Stony Stratford - Woburn (skirting Luton)	18
Woburn - south of Luton	20
South of Luton - St Albans	20
Ipswich - Woodbridge	14
Woodbridge - Blythburgh	25
Blythburgh - Beccles	12
Beccles - south of Norwich	18
South of Norwich - Old Buckenham	20
Old Buckenham - Thetford	18
Thetford - Bury St Edmunds	20
Bury St Edmunds - Newmarket - Cambridge	32
Newton Tony - Chute Causeway	27
Chute Causeway - Lambourn	32
Lambourn - Coleshill	19
Coleshill - Wychwood Forest	25
Wychwood Forest - Chipping Norton	14
Chipping Norton - Broughton Castle	15
Total approximate mileage	1000

Some places to visit

Arrangements do sometimes change and it is as well to check first if you are making a specific journey to visit one of these places:

Amwell Bury, Herts. Not open to the public.

Audley End, Essex. 1 April - 30 September Tuesday - Sunday 1pm - 6pm.

Babraham Hall, Cambs. Not open to the public - occupied by the Animal Physiology Unit of the Agricultural Research Council.

Wandlebury Fort, Cambs. Open all the year.

Cambridge. The buildings known to Celia are generally open to the public all the year and times are displayed at the entrances.

Woolsthorpe Manor, Lincs. April - October Wed - Sun and Bank Holiday Monday 1pm - 5.30pm.

Hinchingbrooke House, Cambs. Now a school, open Sundays.

Elton Hall, near Peterborough. Easter Day & Easter Monday 2pm - 5pm. July - Wednesday & Sunday 2pm - 5pm. August - Wednesday, Thursday & Sunday 2pm - 5pm.

Burghley House, Lincs. Good Friday - 6 October daily 11am - 5pm.

Belton House, Lincs. April - October Wed - Sun and Bank Holiday Monday 1pm - 5.30pm.

Holme Pierrepont, Notts. June, July & August Tuesday, Thursday, Friday, Sunday & Bank Holiday Monday 2pm - 6pm.

Wollaton Hall, Notts. Open all the year 10am - dusk.

Newby Hall, Yorks. Easter - 30 September daily 11am - 5pm.

Welbeck Hall, Notts. Not open to the public.

Chatsworth, Derbyshire. 24 March - 3 November daily 11am - 4.30pm.

Haddon Hall, Derbyshire. Good Friday - 29 September Tuesday - Sunday 11am - 6pm.

Castleton Caves, Derbys. Open to the public.

Shuckburgh House, Warwicks. Not open to the public.

Broughton Castle, Oxfordshire. 14 May - 14 September Wednesday & Sunday plus Thursday July & August plus Bank Holiday Sunday & Monday 2pm - 5pm.

Woburn Abbey, Beds. 25 March - 3 November 11am - 5.30pm daily.

Christchurch Mansion, Suffolk. All the year round Monday - Saturday 10am - 5pm Sunday 2.30pm - 4.30pm.

Roos Hall, Suffolk. Not open to the public.

Euston Park, Suffolk. All the year round Thursday & Sunday.

Cupola House, Bury St Edmunds, Suffolk. A wine bar open to the public.

Littlebury. The home of Henry Winstanley. Long gone.

Bibliography

Travel

The Journeys of Celia Fiennes *ed Christopher Morris 1947*

The Journeys of Celia Fiennes *ed Christopher Morris 1981*

A Tour through England & Wales *Daniel Defoe*

Roads

The Drovers *K J Bonser*

The Icknield Way *Edward Thomas*

Packmen, Carriers & Packhorse Roads *David Hey*

The Old Roads of England *Sir Wm Addison*

Roads & Tracks of Britain *Christopher Taylor*

Roads & Trackways of the Yorkshire Dales *Geoffrey N Wright*

Roman Roads of Britain *Ivan D Margary*

Travel in England in the Seventeenth Century *Joan Parkes*

Landscape

The Making of the English Landscape *W G Hoskins*

The Making of the English Landscape -
Bedfordshire & Huntingdonshire *Peter Bigmore*
Cambridgeshire *Christopher Taylor*
Hertfordshire *Lionel Mumby*
Norfolk *David Dymond*
Northamptonshire *John Steane*
Oxfordshire *Frank Emery*
Shropshire *Trevor Rowley*
Staffordshire *D M Palliser*
Suffolk *Norman Scarfe*

The Making of the English Landscape (contd) -
Yorkshire East Riding *K J Allison*
Yorkshire West Riding *Arthur Rastrick*

Buildings

The English House through Seven Centuries *Olive Cook*

Life in the English Country House *Mark Girouard*

Robert Smythson & the Elizabethan Country House *Mark Girouard*

Gardens

The English Garden *Alan Gore & Laurence Fleming*

The Gardens of William & Mary *David Jacques & Arend Jan vd Horst*

Horses

The Empire of Equus *David P Willoughby*

The Foals of Epona *Antony Dent and Daphne Machin Goodall*

Horses *Elwyn Hartley Edwards*

Horses in Shakespeare's England *Anthony Dent*

The Horse Trade of Tudor and Stuart England *Peter Edwards*

The Royal Horses of Europe *Sylvia Loch*